Winston S. Churchill
Philosopher and Statesman

THE CREDIBILITY OF INSTITUTIONS, POLICIES AND LEADERSHIP
A Series funded by the Hewlett Foundation
Kenneth W. Thompson, *Series Editor*

Winston S. Churchill Philosopher and Statesman

The Credibility of Institutions, Policies and Leadership
Volume 19

Michael Fowler

With a Preface by Kenneth W. Thompson

University Press of America
Lanham • New York • London

Copyright © 1985 by

University Press of America,™ Inc.

4720 Boston Way
Lanham, MD 20706

3 Henrietta Street
London WC2E 8LU England

Co-published by arrangement with
The White Burkett Miller Center of Public Affairs,
The University of Virginia

Library of Congress Cataloging in Publication Data

Fowler, Michael, 1960-
  Winston S. Churchill, philosopher and statesman.

  (The Credibility of institutions, policies and
leadership ; v. 19)
  "Co-published by arrangement with the White Burkett
Miller Center of Public Affairs, the University of
Virginia"—T.p. verso.
  Bibliography: p.
  1. Churchill, Winston, Sir, 1874-1965. 2. Churchill,
Winston, Sir, 1874-1965—Views on international relations.
3. International relations. 4. Statesmen—Great Britain—
Biography. I. White Burkett Miller Center. II. Title.
III. Series.
DA566.9.C5F68   1985   941.082'092'4   84-29122
ISBN 0-8191-4416-9 (alk. paper)
ISBN 0-8191-4417-7 (pbk. : alk. paper)

Contents

Preface

Winston S. Churchill is preeminent among Western leaders and a fitting subject for discussion in an inquiry into leadership. If students of foreign policy were to select one wartime and postwar leader who embodied the qualities most required for leadership, Churchill would be at the head of many lists.

As has been true of other great leaders, his multi-faceted qualities as statesman and philosopher confound those who seek to analyze his leadership. It is possible using carefully selected chapters from his life to describe Churchill's approach to foreign policy in a multitude of ways. I have described Churchill as a realist and would, despite Mr. Michael Fowler's argument, insist that the core of his approach was realistic. Mr. Fowler insists that Churchill was also a romanticist and idealist. He supports this view by showing that Churchill could be flexible which he sees as evidence that Churchill was not a realist while I would argue to the contrary that flexibility is often a necessary requirement of realism. Mr. Fowler has found statements from Churchill in which he expressed doubts about the present day balance of power. I would maintain that throughout his work he emphasizes the continuing relevance of the balance of power. Fowler considers that because Churchill called for superior western power vis-a-vis the Soviet Union that he believed in military superiority rather than political equilibrium. I would urge Mr. Fowler to examine, first, Churchill's statements on superiority (he spoke of a *small* edge over the Soviet Union) and, second, his repeated warnings that not superiority but a political settlement was the one lasting assurance of peace.

I would also ask Mr. Fowler to consider the context in which romanticist and idealist statements were made. Frequently they were put forward for reasons of domestic politics to soothe or inspire the body politic. Other times they were exercises in political rhetoric. The question to be asked of any statesman is what were his policy statements when his nation's vital interests were engaged. Realism may well be subordinated to romanticism or idealism where the nation's survival is not at stake. When national security is threatened, the realist will often set noble ideals aside. In contrast, the true romanticist is not bound by the imperatives of national interest whatever necessity may demand. When he was defending the Yalta agreements before a skeptical Parliament, Churchill made idealistic claims that his fellow realists felt called on to challenge. Yet Churchill as Prime Minister was in search of a broader constituency to support his policies than realists alone comprised.

Having raised a few questions regarding Mr. Fowler's interpretations, I hasten to commend the force and clarity of his study. It is a lively and original work by an impressive and promising young thinker. Further, no one perspective on a leader of the dimensions of Churchill can be sufficient. His experiences are too varied, his responsibilities too diverse and his talents too rich and abundant to give any version of his leadership a monopoly position.

Those who would write on politics or study leadership must assume their views will have their day, however brief, to be supplanted in whole or part by others. The greatest virtue of scholarly imagination is to inspire the imagination of others. Those who come after any group of intellectual historians may build on their work, stand on their shoulders but go beyond it as new sources and ideas come into play. It is for this reason I am pleased that Michael Fowler has made a valuable contribution to the Hewlett Series on Institutions and Leadership by writing on Churchill as Philosopher and Statesman.

Kenneth W. Thompson
White Burkett Miller
Center of Public Affairs

CHAPTER ONE:

Winston Churchill Political Philosopher

I. Introduction: Churchill as Theorist
II. Understanding the International System
III. Approaching the International System in Theory
IV. Approaching the International System in Practice
V. Transforming the International System

INTRODUCTION:

In his superlative memoirs, *Present at the Creation,* Dean Acheson recounted Winston Churchill's visit to Washington in the waning days of the Truman administration. At one point in the proceedings, the Prime Minister paid a courtesy call to the White House and Acheson recalled the following exchange between the two leaders: "The President rather wistfully spoke of how much [he and Mrs. Truman] would enjoy a visit to England but how careful he must be not to do anything that would be misconstrued. The Prime Minister, chuckling, observed that he himself had been misconstrued for fifty years and that no one had really found him out yet."[1]

More than half that time again has passed and no one yet has really 'found out' Winston Churchill. To use his own phrase, the Prime Minister often appears "a riddle wrapped in a mystery inside an enigma." Perhaps the finest piece of recent scholarship on Churchill as political theorist and international statesman, Kenneth W. Thompson's *Winston Churchill's World View: Statesmanship and Power,* construes the Prime Minister to be an early subscriber to the Political Realist philosophy.[2] Alas, even this fine work runs up against the shoals of contrary evidence.

The task of 'finding out' Winston Churchill is made all the more stimulating by the fact that the British leader was a natural schemer, planner, and theorist. In an essay entitled "How to Stop War," written in 1936, Churchill decried the British tendency to try to muddle through crises with a series of ad hoc policies. He wrote: " 'How was it,' the historians of the future will ask, 'that these vast, fairly intelligent, educated and on the whole virtuous communities were so helpless and futile as to allow themselves to become the victims of their own processes, and of what they most abhorred?' The answer will be, 'They had no plan.' "3 Throughout his early career, in Egypt, in India, in South Africa and elsewhere, Churchill entered one controversy after another because he felt that his theory or strategy was more logical, consistent, or clear-sighted than those of his peers.

For all this time and effort devoted to planning, it is not overly surprising that Churchill the statesman put great stock in developing a well-defined theory of international relations. In the first volume of his *History of the Second World War,* Churchill wrote, "It is always more easy to discover and proclaim general principles than to apply them. . . . [However,] those who are possessed of a definite body of doctrine and of deeply rooted convictions upon it will be in a much better position to deal with the shifts and surprises of daily affairs than those who are merely . . . indulging their natural impulses as they are evoked by what they read from day to day."4 On another occasion, speaking of his views on international relations, Churchill remarked, "I try to pursue, as it seems to me, a steady theme and my thought as far as I can grasp it, measure it, is all of one piece."5

Truly, as Henry David Thoreau was wont to say, "It is as hard to see oneself as to look backwards without turning." Churchill's international theorizing, to some at least, may have been worthy of much praise. It was hardly, however, "all of one piece." Indeed, the various, often seemingly contradictory, theoretical positions that Churchill espoused have confounded analysts of his thought. Yet, to label Churchill's political philosophy an amalgam is to point to a certain theoretical discontinuity, but also to a helpful degree of practical flexibility. Particularly in his Cold War dealings, Churchill could measure his company and apply his theory accordingly.

If Churchill's amalgamated philosophy implies a singular and independent approach to the issues of the day, this is as it should be. When those about him were mired in gloom at the prospects presented in the international scene, Churchill was often at his most hopeful. Similarly, when the optimists reigned, Churchill was at his most cautiously pessimistic. As a result, the wartime Prime Minister often saw beyond the scholarly fads of the day. He was taken in neither by euphoria at the prospects of the United Nations, nor by fatalism at the prospects of an endless Cold War. He was cautious about the chances for continued Allied amity after World War Two, but he was equally doubtful that nuclear holocaust was inevitable. The Prime Minister delighted in embracing the minority side of debates on international relations. As he proudly put it in his early autobiography, "All through my life I have found myself in disagreement alternately with both the historic English parties. . . . Thus I have always been against the Pacifists during the quarrel and against the Jingoes at its close."[6]

Not only was Churchill's analysis rarely swayed by current fashions, but, perhaps as a consequence, his words were often remarkably prescient. Otto von Bismarck once remarked, "Political genius consists of hearing the distant hoofbeat of the horse of history and then leaping to catch the passing horseman by the coattails."[7] Astonishingly often, Churchill was in prime position waiting for that horseman of history to gallop by. His book entitled *Step By Step 1936–1939* stands as a monument to an exceedingly acute vision of the future. If prophecy is indeed, in Walter Lippmann's words, "seeing the necessary amidst confusion and insignificance,"[8] then on occasion Churchill was surely prophetic.

For all its acuteness in certain regards, Churchill's theory was not the slightest bit orthodox. In reconstructing his political philosophy, then, perhaps the best method is to break down Churchill's ideas into several component parts—understanding the international system, approaching the international system in theory and practice, and, finally, transforming the international system. Constructed systematically in this manner, the portrait of Churchill which eventually emerges on our canvas is one that bears little resemblance to the hard-nosed Political Realist many assume the British leader to have been.

UNDERSTANDING THE INTERNATIONAL SYSTEM:

Churchill was under absolutely no delusions about the primary role which the possession and the use of force play in the international drama. The system must be understood, the Prime Minister felt, to be based in the first instance on power relationships. In 1936 Churchill proclaimed, "Sentiment by itself is no good; fine speeches are worse than useless; short-sighted optimism is a mischief; smooth, soothing platitudes are a crime. . . . No plan for stopping war . . . is of any value unless it has behind it force, and the resolve to use that force."[9] In Churchill's views rests no hint of the utopian notion that the fact of force is in itself a great defect of the international community. After all, as the Prime Minister put it, "The scales of Justice are vain without her sword."[10]

Indeed, Churchill regularly indicated that the drama of international politics was most often played out in terms of the strong and the weak. Here too, of course, he was well within the bounds of Realist dogma. "This abyss of inequities which we call politics," Churchill once colorfully remarked, "is vainly covered with a tissue of brilliant phrases. It is easy for anyone of the least intelligence . . . to see through this tissue and recognize that in spite of evangelical treaties, and in spite of a reign of justice, it is always the weaker who are sacrificed to the interests of the more powerful."[11]

Similarly, in debate before Parliament in 1945 over the United Nations framework being constructed at Dumbarton Oaks, a pacifist Labour M.P. stated that there was no method in the proposed Charter to deal with aggression by a Great Power. Churchill dryly replied, "I am sorry that there should be a high degree of axiomatic truth in the fact stated by the hon. Member."[12] A few moments later he continued: "We may deplore, if we choose, the fact that there is a difference between great and small, between the strong and the weak in the world, but there undoubtedly is such a difference, and it would be foolish to upset good arrangements . . . for the sake of trying to obtain immediately what is a hopeless ideal."

To the theorist, inequality of power in the international system is customarily assessed as not an entirely unmitigated evil. Hedley Bull, for instance, has argued convincingly that variances in the power of states are of cardinal importance in keeping order within the system. In *The Anarchical Society,* Bull wrote, "Because states are grossly unequal in power, certain international issues are as a consequence settled, the demands of certain states (weak ones) can in practice be left out of account, the demands of certain other states (strong ones) recognized to be the only ones relevant to the issue at hand."[13]

Churchill made the same point about the positive effect of unequal power in several different contexts. In a speech in Brussels in November 1945, while denying that the era of small states was over, the Prime Minister emphasized the transcendent importance of the Great Powers in securing peace for all.[14] Similarly, Churchill understood this principle to be at work in postwar Poland. He put extraordinary pressure on the London Poles to accept the reality both of their weak bargaining position and of the nature of the world in which they lived. At one point, Averell Harriman reported, Churchill told Polish leader Stanislaw Mikolajczyk: "We are not going to wreck the peace of Europe because of quarrels between Poles. . . . Unless you accept the frontier you are out of business forever. The Russians will sweep through your country and your people will be liquidated. You are on the verge of annihilation."[15] While unequal power might regrettably work injustices on a people such as the Poles, Churchill believed that unequal power, if acknowledged, might also provide the foundation for a peaceful Europe.

The notion of inequality of power and its effect on international order also influenced Churchill's views of imperialism. Rupert Emerson has written, "Denunciation of imperialism in terms of its primary purpose of promoting the interests of the few advanced powers should not be allowed to obscure its role as a principal pillar of the world order of its day."[16] Undeniably, Churchill was first and foremost a romantic imperialist, a great oak surviving from a Victorian forest. "I have not become Prime Minister," Churchill would thunder dramatically, "to preside over the liquidation of the British Empire."[17] But Churchill also understood and tried to justify imperialism in the language of international order. Through the great parliamentary battles of the 1930s over British policy in India, Churchill vehemently insisted that order was fundamentally at stake. In his view the stronger powers were responsible for taking a lead in maintaining stability, and, in fact, for enforcing a great power collective hegemonial peace. As Churchill explained in 1930, "When eagles are silent, parrots begin to jabber."[18]

Hand in hand with his views on the duty of the Great Powers to keep order was Churchill's conception of spheres of influence. Martin Wight has defined the term in the following manner: "A sphere of interest is one where an international police authority is assumed by the presiding power and exercised by means of intervention."[19] Plainly, the notion of unequal power contributing to world order dovetails neatly with the idea of spheres of influence. Hedley Bull explained it this way, "Great powers contribute to international order not only by unilaterally exploiting their preponderance in particular areas of the world or among particular groups of states, but also by agreeing to establish spheres of influence, interest, or responsibility."[20]

Churchill's concept of regionalism, a concept that will merit further discussion, was clearly based on the premise that spheres of influence can have a salutary effect in keeping international order. Churchill believed, throughout the war years as well as during the postwar period, that stability might be insured by a division of the globe into several grand spheres of influence. Within each of these regions, a Great Power or, presumably, a Great Concert of Powers, would keep the peace. In practice, of course, Churchill employed the sphere concept in his celebrated percentage agreement with Stalin on southeastern Europe, though the efficacy of the arrangement, for all its publicity, is open to serious question.[21]

As previously noted, Churchill's personal theory of international relations, composed as it was of an amalgam of Realist, romanticist, and idealist elements, gave the Prime Minister the ability to measure his company and apply accordingly the most effective theoretical precept under the circumstances. In dealing with the Soviets, of whom was once remarked, "The Russians are nothing if not realists,"[22] Churchill naturally relied heavily on his own principles of Realism. Primary among these was the idea that power is an essential tool in confronting international adversaries.

In a speech in New York in 1949, Churchill put his views down bluntly: "You have not only to convince the Soviet Government that you have superior force—that they are confronted by superior force—but that you are not restrained by any moral consideration if the case arose from using that force with complete material ruthlessness. And that is the greatest chance of peace, the surest road to peace."[23] Again, in April 1945, when arguing in favor of a push eastward into Germany by the Allied forces, Churchill wrote to Franklin Roosevelt: "I believe this is the best chance of saving the future. If they [the Soviets] are convinced that we are afraid of them and can be bullied into submission, then indeed I should despair of our future relations with them and much else."[24]

Given the power-oriented basis of the international system, Churchill was not hesitant to employ force for primarily political ends. In the post-Yalta period, he strongly advised the Allies, as Maxwell Schoenfeld summarized, "to employ the policy of using military forces to secure positions of strength from which to negotiate with the Soviets on the central German front."[25] The Allied Command was not often disposed to accept his advice in this regard. Nevertheless, when Churchill had a free strategic hand—as in dealing with Communist partisans in Greece and Brussels—he unswervingly put his principles of Realism to practice.

Furthermore, Winston Churchill was far from unduly vexed at the prospect of life in the nuclear age. In fact, the Prime Minister was wholeheartedly in favor of nuclear weapons insofar as they constituted a formidable deterrent to major convulsions in the international order. In 1953 Churchill told Parliament:

> It may be that . . . when the advance of destructive weapons enables everyone to kill everybody else nobody will want to kill anyone at all.
>
> At any rate, it seems pretty safe to say that a war which begins by both sides suffering what they dread most, and that is undoubtedly the case at present, is less likely to occur than one which dangles the lurid prizes of former ages before ambitious eyes.[26]

Churchill himself saw his position on nuclear weapons as eminently realistic. "Moralists may find it a melancholy thought," he once observed, "that peace can find no nobler foundation than mutual terror. But for my part, I shall be content if these foundations are solid, because they will give us the extra time and the new breathing space for the supreme effort which has to be made for a world settlement."[27] The Prime Minister believed strongly in the efficacy of deterrence: the sterner the penalty, the less likely the aggression. In 1940 Churchill stated, "I have always held the view that the maintenance of peace depends upon the accumulation of deterrents against aggression."[28] In March 1950 he expanded on this theme saying, "There never was a time when the deterrents against aggression were so strong. If penalties of the most drastic kind can prevent in our civil life crime or folly, then we certainly have them here on a gigantic scale in the affairs of nations."[29]

This great concern for the magnitude of the deterrent accounts for Churchill's vehement hostility to early proposals for a 'no-first-use' doctrine.[30] It also helps to explain his reluctance to share nuclear secrets with the Kremlin. First, Churchill believed there were no great gains to be had from early nuclear cooperation and consultation with the Soviets. At one point he argued before the House of Commons:

> We are told by those who advocate immediate public disclosure that the Soviet Government are already possessed of the scientific knowledge, and that they will be able to make atomic bombs in a very short time. This, I may point out, is somewhat inconsistent with the argument that they have a grievance, and also with the argument for what it is worth, that we and the United States have at this moment any great gift to bestow, such as would induce a complete melting of hearts and create some entirely new relationship.[31]

Second, the Prime Minister believed there was a great potential disadvantage. Early in the war effort, the British leader voiced his concern that the Soviets would pose a serious threat to the stability of the postwar international order. This threat, in Churchill's view, might well be neutralized by a strong nuclear deterrent. In 1948 he observed, "The atomic bomb . . . alone at the present time prevents the rebarbarization and enslavement of Europe by the Communist forces directed from the Kremlin."[32]

As time passed, Churchill grew almost euphoric in cataloguing the positive attributes of nuclear weaponry. At one point, Robert Osgood and Robert W. Tucker note, Churchill went so far as to claim that the tremendous destructive capacity of nuclear weapons might end war, at least war among the major powers. As the Prime Minister remarked, "It may well be that we shall, by a process of sublime irony, have reached a stage in this story where safety will be the sturdy child of terror, and survival the twin brother of anarchy."[33] Indeed, in 1955 Churchill exclaimed, "It is to the universality of potential destruction that we may look with hope and even confidence."[34] And, one might observe, almost thirty years have passed and Churchill's thesis has yet to be firmly disproven.

All told, Winston Churchill understood the international system to be based primarily on power. This was a milieu in which he felt very much at home. "The pursuit of power," the Prime Minister once remarked, "with the capacity and the desire to exercise it worthily is among the noblest of human occupations."[35] Without much doubt, this view of the world is the portion of Churchill's political philosophy which most closely approximates the thought of the Political Realist school. However, to say that Churchill understood the function of force in international relations cannot in and of itself make a Realist out of him. Woodrow Wilson, too, understood the realities of power in the world as is attested to by his actions in Mexico and Europe and a variety of his postwar statements.[36] However, the Realist school shuns the American president. The true division between Political Realists and idealists, one might contend, is not in the realization of the importance of power in relations among states, most statesmen get this far, but instead is in the uses and direction to which one advocates that power be channelled. With this in mind, let us turn to how Churchill proposed that Britain survive in this hostile international system. Here, the argument that Churchill's philosophy was Realist through and through begins to founder.

APPROACHING THE INTERNATIONAL SYSTEM IN THEORY

In early 1944, Winston Churchill remarked to Baroness Asquith: "I realized at Teheran for the first time what a small nation we are. There I sat with the great Russian bear on one side of me, with paws outstretched . . . and, on the other, the great American buffalo, and between the two sat the poor little British donkey, who was the only one of the three who knew the right way home."[37] What was this elusive 'right way home'? Given that the international community, according to Churchill, is fundamentally based on the possession and use of force, the strong against the weak, and devil take the hindmost, how does a country survive in the system? What were the prescriptions for national security as Churchill saw them?

What were the major alternatives that, in his mind, the system offered?

Naturally, when a man who emphasized power in international relations turned to the subject of security and survival in the system, he would again be likely to stress the need to gather force against potential adversaries. This, in fact, was Winston Churchill's approach. In 1936 Churchill told Parliament, "I am looking for peace. I am looking for a way to stop war, but you will not stop it by pious sentiments and appeals. You will only stop it by practical arrangements."[38] Plainly, this attitude opens up a host of other questions. Churchill was decidedly in favor of accumulating deterrents to stop aggression, yet many different methods might be employed toward this end. Which method of accumulating deterrents did Churchill favor? Why did he believe that method in particular would ensure, or at least contribute to, international order? Finally, what school of international theorists champions Churchill's favored method? In what tradition of scholarly thought on this subject might Churchill be placed?

In his *Power in International Relations,* Inis Claude has developed a useful schema for categorizing approaches to power. He took the three cardinal concepts in the field—balance of power, collective security, and world government—and observed that the first involves extreme, almost laissez-faire, decentralization of power; the second involves partially centralized management of power; and the third involves a complete monopoly of power. Claude concluded, "My central hypothesis is that these concepts—balance of power, collective security, and world government—are related to each other as successive points along a continuum, differing most fundamentally in the degree of centralization of power and authority which they imply."[39] In the remainder of our discussion in this subsection, let us examine Churchill's thoughts on the first two concepts and reserve for our treatment of "Transforming the International System" his thoughts on world government. Throughout the chapter, the point will be developed that the farther one moves down the Claude continuum away from balance of power and toward world government, the more difficult it is to justify one's approach in terms of the precepts of Political Realism.

The use of the term 'balance of power' among statesmen and academicians is notoriously problematic. The multiple meanings which different people ascribe to the word, indeed sometimes which the same person ascribes to the word, bedevil the historian.[40] No doubt, through his long career in public service, Churchill was no more consistent than anyone else in referring to the 'balance of power'. However, during the years that most directly concern us, those just before, during, and after World War II, Churchill made absolutely clear his reservations about reliance on the balance of power concept in what might be termed its classical form.

Emmerich de Vattel set forth a classical definition of balance of power when he referred to it as "a state of affairs such that no one power is in a position where it is preponderant and can lay down the law to others."[41] Robert Osgood and Robert W. Tucker proceeded along broadly similar lines in stating, "The prerequisite of order among autonomous states is that force be restrained by countervailing force within a balance (or equilibrium) of power."[42] The idea in the classical view is that when equal force confronts equal force, peace will reign since no side has the upper hand in the power relationship.

The ambiguities in Churchill's writing on the classical version of the balance of power permit two interpretations. He might have believed that the classical balance once worked reasonably effectively but no longer could. Alternatively, he might have believed that the only balance of power that had proven effective over the ages was not a balance, strictly speaking, but was a preponderance of force 'balanced' or directed against an ambitious aggressor. Whichever interpretation is correct, Churchill certainly did not believe the classical balance of power was the solution to security problems in the interwar and Cold War periods.

The first interpretation, that the classical balance of power was outdated by the latter half of the twentieth century, is suggested by Churchill in his celebrated Fulton, Missouri address in 1946. The former Prime Minister stated:

> From what I have seen of our Russian friends and Allies during the war, I am convinced that there is nothing they admire so much as strength, and there is nothing for which they have less respect than for weakness, especially military weakness. For that reason the old doctrine of a balance of power is unsound. We cannot afford, if we can help it, to work on narrow margins, offering temptations to a trial of strength.[43]

On other occasions, the second interpretation, that a classical balance had never worked effectively, seems more in accord with Churchill's words. Before Parliament in 1934, Churchill set forth this presumably timeless principle: "If you wish to bring about war, you bring about such an equipoise that both sides think they have a chance of winning. If you want to stop war, you gather such an aggregation of force on the side of peace that the aggressor, whoever he may be, will not dare to challenge."[44] In this same vein, Churchill voiced the following precept in 1947: "Great wars come when both sides believe they are more or less equal, when each thinks it has a good chance of victory."[45]

Churchill's most famous reference to the balance of power came in a speech in March 1936 which he later quoted in *The Gathering Storm* and in which he called the balance of power "the wonderful unconscious tradition of British foreign policy."[46] Yet, again, Churchill was not defending a classical balance of power at all; rather, he was defending the need to confront a European aggressor with a preponderance of force. The Prime Minister wrote:

> Faced by Philip II of Spain, against Louis XIV under William III and Marlborough, against Napoleon, against William II of Germany, it would have been very tempting to join with the stronger and share the fruits of conquest. However, we always took the harder course, joined with the less strong Powers, made a combination among them, and thus defeated and frustrated the Continental military tyrant whoever he was, whatever nation he led.[47]

Churchill's concern with rallying different states to present a preponderance of force against a potential aggressor was also evident throughout the postwar period. In telegrams to President Truman as well as in orders to his own troops, Churchill stressed the danger posed by the clear superiority in conventional forces which the Soviets would enjoy after American withdrawal and British demobilization. On May 27, 1945 Churchill wrote to Major-General Sir Hastings Ismay, "I do not wish to be left alone with no troops at all and great Russian masses free to do whatever they choose in Europe."[48] Churchill's fear was not simply of Russian preponderance of force; he was concerned even at the prospect of equal forces in the two blocs. Claude has observed:

Churchill betrayed no love of equipoise when he said to Stalin, in 1945: 'There is not much comfort in looking into a future where you and the countries you dominate, plus the Communist Parties in many other states, are all drawn up on one side, and those who rally to the English-speaking nations and their associates or Dominions are on the other. It is quite obvious that their quarrel would tear the world to pieces.'[49]

What all this demonstrates is that the only way Churchill can be made out to be a balance of power advocate is to use the term in the loose sense of a preponderance of power against a potential aggressor. But when employed so vaguely, balance of power can be made out to be almost a sister term to collective security. After all, collective security, too, sets forth a method of welding together large forces to oppose an adversary. If correct in presuming that Churchill's balance of power was of the preponderance and not the classical mode, we might expect to find the Prime Minister endorsing collective security. In fact, Churchill specifically and enthusiastically promoted the concept of collective security on any number of occasions. The implications of this endorsement cast a grave shadow on Churchill's credentials as a Political Realist.

One formulation of the collective security concept postulates that every country might contribute equally to stopping aggression anywhere in the world. Churchill was too shrewd to believe this type of commitment was workable.[50] Nevertheless, he did insist that a graduated zonal response to collective security was a perfectly viable alternative. He wrote in 1936:

In the front line, pledged to all the necessary measures, well equipped, strictly combined, stand those who dwell nearest to the Potential Aggressor; in the second line those likely to be next affected, or indirectly affected, by his aggression. Farther off, and least heavily committed, will be the States who, while they do not fear this particular Potential Aggressor, nevertheless realize that some day in a different set of circumstances, their turn may come.[51]

Similarly, on July 11, 1937, Churchill again advocated using collective security as a method of gathering preponderant force.

He predicted, "Evidently we are approaching the point where the League of Nations, if properly supported, will have an immense and perhaps decisive part to play in the prevention of a brutal trial of strength. How else are we going to marshal adequate and if possible overwhelming forces against brazen, unprovoked aggression, except by a grand alliance of peace-seeking peoples under the authority of an august international body?"[52]

In the aftermath of World War Two, Churchill's faith in the collective security option was still quite robust. In *The Gathering Storm* Churchill observed, "The argument [for collective security] is not necessarily without its application today."[53] On March 31, 1949, the British leader declared:

> There was of course one way to prevent [the world wars] —one way then as now—the creation of an international instrument strong enough to adjust the disputes of nations and enforce its decisions against an aggressor. . . .
>
> [T]he statesmen of Versailles, largely at the inspiration of President Wilson, an inspiration implemented effectively by British thought, created the League of Nations. This is their defense before history, and had the League been resolutely sustained and used, it would have saved us all.[54]

How does Churchill's advocacy of collective security cast doubt on his credentials as a Political Realist? First, it is important to understand that collective security, properly conceived, is anything but a sister of balance of power, properly conceived. Arnold Wolfers explained the collective security concept this way:

> What exponents of the principle of collective security have in mind is to urge nations to change the customary direction of their defense policy. They call upon them to go beyond aligning themselves with one another only to meet threats emanating from common enemies and instead to embrace a policy of defense against aggression in general or, more precisely, against any aggressor anywhere.[55]

Wolfers correctly pointed out that collective security and balance of power are in no way synonymous terms, though both aim at halting aggression. He wrote, " 'Collective security' . . . assumes that the peace of the world depends not on having the power of all nations balanced and checked by the power of others but, on the contrary, on making overwhelming power available to those who are ready to oppose potential aggressor nations or to punish actual aggressors."[56] Churchill doubtless was attracted to the theory of collective security because it corresponded so nicely with his own conviction that potential aggressors must be met by a preponderance of force.

To the Realists, collective security is anathema. In a book which has become a major tenet of the Political Realist faith, Kenneth W. Thompson has written, "Collective security in practice has been hampered by . . . persistent problems, all stemming from one fundamental source. In a word this source is the fatal divorce of the theory from political reality."[57] Indeed, the great attacks on Woodrow Wilson by the Realists more often than not cite Wilson's support for collective security as an example of his unrealistic Idealist view of the world. What card-carrying Realist could in good conscience support an approach to power that requires wholesale changes in the foreign policy of states, that requires the subordination of immediate national interests to potential long-term gains, that requires great faith in an international organization, and that divides the world into 'aggressor' and 'peace-loving' nations?

This categorizing, or stereotyping, of nations, indicates a further rift between Churchill and the Realists. Louis Halle has written:

> For the American and the British people, . . . the War was simply a struggle between the forces of good and the forces of evil. . . .
>
> In this mythology of a world divided between 'peace-loving' and 'aggressor' nations it was, by definition, the nature of 'peace-loving' nations always to love peace and of 'aggressor' nations always to aggress.[58]

Halle goes on to argue convincingly that the Allied leaders allowed this conception of the world to guide their wartime policy toward Germany, in particular, their policy of unconditional surrender. This objective of utterly destroying German power was adopted with little regard for the obvious next question: which power would fill the vacuum thus created.[59] In Halle's view, the process of vacuum-filling led inexorably to Cold War confrontation.

In the following chapter, we shall examine the issue of Churchill and the policy of unconditional surrender in some detail; for now, suffice it to say that, at minimum, the Prime Minister never repudiated publicly the policy during the war years and never divorced the distinction between 'peace-loving' and 'aggressor' nations from his own thought. Indeed, is not this attitude on Churchill's part perfectly consistent with his philosophical bent? Arnold Wolfers has pointed out that collective security, also, is based on the same rather simplistic division of peace-loving and aggressor nations. Wolfers explained that there is no great fear about the possible problems inherent in granting the 'peace-loving' nations so much unrestrained power: "By the rules of collective security, the 'peace-loving nations' of the world cannot have too much power since they can be expected never to abuse their supremacy."[60]

These notions, fundamental assumptions of collective security doctrine, stand as one of the chief reasons that Political Realists have been reluctant to embrace the theory. Given Churchill's advocacy of collective security theory and given his implicit agreement with the view of the world which underlies the theory (corroborated by his support for policies such as unconditional surrender), it is indeed peculiar that the Realists seem so eager to take Churchill as one of their own. Inis Claude has provided a clue to understanding this paradox in noting "the widespread tendency to make balance of power a symbol of realism, and hence of respectability, for the scholar or statesman."[61] Perhaps the Realists have taken Churchill's favorable references to the balance of power at face value, without focusing on the Prime Minister's usage of the term and concomitant support for the collective security alternative.

APPROACHING THE INTERNATIONAL SYSTEM IN PRACTICE

A conservative internationally as well as domestically, Winston Churchill uniformly favored marshalling deterrents against disorder. In a sentence, the Prime Minister's views might be summarized as follows: the more preponderant the deterrent, the better the prospects for a stable international order. The theoretical alternative which seemed most likely to aggregate disparate forces into a formidable deterrent was, in Churchill's mind, collective security. On the purely theoretical level, this was the approach to power Churchill most favored.

When approaching the international system in practice, however, Churchill recognized that the art of statesmanship required a good deal more than proselytizing for different theoretical paths toward maintaining world order. For instance, the Prime Minister put great stock in the complementary use of diplomacy and negotiation between potential adversaries. Far from "an honest man sent abroad to lie for his country," as some would have it, the diplomat was, to Churchill, the master figure in preventing future disasters. "Most wars in history," Churchill once remarked, "have been avoided simply by postponing them."[62] The primary job of the diplomat was to mute antagonistic interests, or at least to delay hostilities, in hopes of finding a reasonable settlement.

Hedley Bull has identified several major functions of diplomacy: to facilitate communication between states, to gather information to aid in forming foreign policy, and to negotiate agreements based on overlapping interests.[63] Churchill's thoughts on diplomacy fit well into this framework. He always believed, for example, that communication between states was of vital practical importance. "The reason for having diplomatic relations," he liked to say, "is not to confer a compliment, but to secure a convenience."[64] Hence, important as was having diplomatic relations with steadfast friends, it was of even more transcendent importance to have diplomatic relations with potential adversaries.

As for the fact-finding function of diplomacy, in a colorful passage in a speech in 1946, Churchill criticized Soviet diplomacy for its poor gathering of information as well as its lack of interest in negotiating a diplomatic settlement. Churchill wryly observed:

> The handful of very able men who hold 180 million Soviet citizens in their grasp ought to be able to get better advice about the Western democracies. For instance, it cannot be in the interests of Russia to go on irritating the United States. There are no people in the world who are so slow to develop hostile feelings against a foreign country as the Americans, and there are no people in the world who, once estranged, are more difficult to win back.

> The American eagle sits on his perch, a large, strong bird
> with formidable beak and claws. There he sits motionless,
> and M. Gromyko is sent day after day to prod him with a
> sharp stick—now his neck, now under his wings, now his
> tail feathers. All the time the eagle keeps quite still. But it
> would be a great mistake to suppose that nothing is going
> on inside the breast of the eagle. I venture to give this
> friendly hint to my old wartime comrade, Marshal Stalin.[65]

As for Bull's third function of diplomacy, Churchill believed
strongly not only that there were overlapping interests between the
western allies and the Soviet Union in the postwar period, but also
that agreements with communists were meaningful. Churchill's
faith in diplomacy was unwavering, despite his grave doubts as to
the general trustworthiness of the leaders in the Kremlin. Harriman
reported: "Referring to the Russians, Churchill said they had no
understanding of such words as 'honesty,' 'honor,' 'trust,' and
'truth'—in fact that they regarded these as negative virtues. They
will, he said, try every door in the house, enter all the rooms which
are not locked, and when they come to one that is barred, if they
are unsuccessful in breaking through it they will withdraw and
invite you to dine genially that same evening."[66] While Churchill
might well count his spoons every evening, however, he would not
shut the Russians out of the house.

Churchill's mistrust of the Soviet leadership was matched inch
for inch by the Russians' mistrust of the Prime Minister. Yugoslav
leader Milovan Djilas reported Stalin as saying:

> Perhaps you think just because we are the allies of the
> English that we have forgotten who they are and who
> Churchill is. They find nothing sweeter than to trick their
> allies. During the First World War they constantly tricked
> the Russians and the French. And Churchill? Churchill is
> the kind who, if you don't watch him, will slip a kopeck
> out of your pocket. Yes, a kopeck out of your pocket! By
> God, a kopeck out of your pocket! And Roosevelt?
> Roosevelt is not like that. He dips his hand only for bigger
> coins. But Churchill? Churchill—even a kopeck.[67]

But even despite this deep-seated mutual antagonism, Churchill
vehemently and consistently counselled trying to reach agreement
with Moscow. In a speech delivered on January 23, 1948, he said,

"It is idle to reason or argue with the Communists. It is, however, possible to deal with them on a fair, realistic basis, and, in my experience, they will keep their bargains as long as it is in their interests to do so, which might, in this grave matter, be a long time once things were settled."[68]

In fact, Churchill so consistently stressed the importance of negotiating a diplomatic settlement with the Russians that it is difficult to find a major address critical of the Soviet Union that did not simultaneously hold out an olive branch of one sort or another. While the speech at Fulton drew attention for its Iron Curtain phrase and its hostile reception in Moscow, perhaps the primary theme of Churchill's words was that a diplomatic settlement was vitally important: "Our difficulties and dangers will not be removed by closing our eyes to them. They will not be removed by mere waiting to see what happens; nor will they be removed by a policy of appeasement. What is needed is a settlement, and the longer this is delayed, the more difficult it will be and the greater our dangers will become."[69]

"Politics," Woodrow Wilson once remarked, "is the slow boring of hard wood."[70] When Churchill claimed the British donkey "knew the right way home," he had in mind no astonishing shortcut, no magic innovation, no international sleight of hand. As Churchill told his fellow Conservatives in October 1948, "I will not encourage you . . . with false hopes of a speedy and friendly settlement with Soviet Russia. It may be that some formula will be found or some artificial compromise effected which will be hailed as a solution and deliverance. But the fundamental danger and antagonisms will remain."[71] The 'right way home' involved, most basically, the accumulation of deterrents against aggression complemented always by the steadfast and vigilant use of the diplomatic art.

But for Churchill, the 'right way home' demanded also the realization that world politics, while certainly oriented toward relationships based on power, is not guided exclusively by national interests narrowly or selfishly defined. The Prime Minister believed that some nations in some circumstances are guided by idealistic, even romantic, impulses. And, in his mind, this state of affairs was normal, understandable, and laudable. Yet, although Churchill was in part an idealist, he was an idealist unafraid to temper his idealism with pragmatism. Hans Morgenthau has quoted Churchill as saying, "The human race cannot make progress without idealism, but idealism at other people's expense and without regard to the consequences of ruin and slaughter which fall upon millions of humble homes cannot be considered as its highest or noblest form."[72] Yet, it would be equally erroneous to see the pragmatist but to miss the idealist. In March 1938 Churchill told the House of Commons: "There must be a moral basis for British rearmament and foreign policy."[73]

On the one hand, the British Prime Minister would characteristically exclaim, "What are we going to have between the white snows of Russia and the white cliffs of Dover?"[74] On the other hand, it was just as typical for him to caution, "It is a great mistake to suppose that nations are not led by sentiment."[75] Churchill was a statesman who understood power politics, but who refused to confine either his analyses of, or his actions in, the international arena to the terms of Realpolitik. "The airlift into Berlin," Churchill proclaimed, "has won the heart of Germany—gathered the heart of Germany over to us—as nothing else could have done and shown them that their choice should be with the Western Nations and with progress and with freedom."[76]

Similarly, as one of the great romanticists of the twentieth century, Churchill was quick to identify the romantic element in the foreign policies of states. The twin themes of conscience and duty run throughout Churchill's comments on how best to approach the international system. "A nation without conscience," he once observed, "is a nation without soul. A nation without soul is a nation that cannot live."[77] On the occasion of Neville Chamberlain's death, Churchill spoke of the judgments history makes of statesmen and of the guideposts statesmen should follow:

> History with its flickering lamp stumbles along the trail of the past, trying to reconstruct its scenes, to revive its echoes, and kindle with pale gleams the passion of former days. What is the worth of all this? The only guide to a man is his conscience; the only shield to his memory is the rectitude and sincerity of his actions. It is very imprudent to walk through life without this shield, because we are so often mocked by the failure of our hopes and the upsetting of our calculations; but with this shield, however the fates may play, we march always in the ranks of honour.[78]

In the same mode, Churchill once commented, "The only wise course is to follow the course of duty and not of interest. Every man knows what his duty is. But it is not given to many to know their true interest."[79]

Lest one mistakenly suppose that these admonitions to follow conscience and duty were not meant by Churchill to apply to the rough-and-tumble of international politics, take note of the Prime Minister's May 1946 speech describing Britain's entry into World War Two. Churchill pronounced in a Wilsonian passage:

> We ... drew the sword against the mighty antagonist at the call of honour and in defence of the rights of weaker nations, according to our plighted word, according to the fair play of the world. We did not fight only in the sacred cause of self-defence. ... We fought for a higher and broader theme. We fought against tyranny, aggression and broken faith, and in order to establish that rule of law among nations which alone can be the shield of freedom and progress.[80]

Doubtless, this romantic streak contributed to Churchill's outspoken opposition, criticized by Anthony Eden among others, to any British territorial gains from the war.[81]

The belief that in certain circumstances there was a good deal more to international statesmanship than raw power politics more than once afforded Churchill a breadth and acuteness of vision beyond that of his Realist contemporaries. At the same time, however, his trust that states might radically change the thrust of their foreign policies occasionally led the British Prime Minister astray. This was so in the case of Yalta and the Soviets.

In his portrait of Churchill as a Political Realist *par excellence,* Kenneth W. Thompson has discounted the Prime Minister's justification of the Yalta agreement as a politically expedient cover for an inherently realistic policy.[82] The evidence permits a different interpretation. First, the question arises whether or not defending Yalta as a morally just settlement to which the Soviets might be expected to adhere was in fact politically expedient, or, indeed, if Churchill even believed it to be expedient. If the defense were merely a ploy designed to win votes in Parliament, it could only have been based on a profound political misjudgment. Churchill was assailed from both sides in the parliamentary debate and the decisive votes were turned toward support of the agreement not by Churchill's idealism, but by the realistic interpretation offered by Churchill's colleagues, notably Captain Peter Thorneycroft. One Member of Parliament commented after the debate, "One thing is certain, however great the vote may be today, it will not be because they believe the motion was just."[83]

Alternatively, if the idealistic justification were aimed at the larger British public, it is unclear why Churchill chose this issue to stray from his generally straight-shooting style. On many other difficult issues Churchill was unafraid to speak his mind even when his thoughts may not have been politically helpful. To select only a few of myriad examples, Churchill shunned the politically beneficial route in stressing to the British public that their country must play a secondary role of supporting the United States in the 1950s, in blasting the popular policies of appeasement in the interwar period, and in emphasizing the great Soviet thrust in the immediate postwar era. As the Prime Minister himself observed, "People who are not prepared to do unpopular things and to defy clamour are not fit to be Ministers in times of stress."[84] Had Churchill truly believed that the Yalta agreement was a sham, bound to founder on the rocks of Realistic power politics, it is hardly implausible to expect him to say so publicly.

Even if Churchill did balk at a public disavowal of Yalta, it seems incredible that he did not express his supposedly great misgivings privately or confidentially. In fact, Churchill appears genuinely pleased by Yalta throughout the Confidential Annexes to the War Cabinet Minutes. At one point, the Minutes were reported as follows: "So far as Premier Stalin is concerned, [Churchill] was quite sure that he meant well to the world and to Poland. He did not himself think that there would be any resentment on the part of Russia about the arrangements that had been made for free and fair elections in that country."[85] Similarly, when Prime Minister Peter Fraser of New Zealand telegraphed Churchill with certain criticisms of the Yalta Agreement, the British Prime Minister replied, "It is my good hopes that Russia, or at any rate Stalin, desired [sic] to work in harmony with the Western Democracies."[86]

Thus we see that while Churchill was far from blind to the role of power in international relations, he was equally far from standing cheek by jowl with the dogmatic Political Realists. His theoretical approach to international politics was marked by an enthusiasm for the concept of collective security that was, at minimum, highly unseemly for a Realistic statesman. Moreover, his practical approach to international politics included an idealistic, indeed romantic, strain eschewed by the Realist school. Let us complete our picture of Churchill's theory of international relations by turning to a final non-Realistic element—the Prime Minister's thoughts on transforming the international system.

TRANSFORMING THE INTERNATIONAL SYSTEM

Winston Churchill, good Tory that he was, tended to shy from making grandiose predictions about how the world might change. As he said at the Massachusetts Institute of Technology, "I was so glad that . . . you asked me to talk about the past rather than to peer into the future, because I know more about the past than I do about the future."[87] Still, over the years, Churchill was persuaded to do "a little peering" and did contemplate on occasion how the international system might change.

Again, the Prime Minister's vision of future international politics was not in close accord with that of most Political Realists. The problem is not that the Realists deny that great changes in the international system might take place, though one might well ask how radical any transformations can possibly be if all statesmen "think and act in terms of interest defined as power."[88] The real problem is that Realists claim radical transformations can only come about 'their way': "through the workmanlike manipulation of the perennial forces that have shaped the past."[89] Churchill's 'one-fell-swoop' approach to international change hardly corresponds with Realist doctrine.

Of the various modifications which Churchill foresaw in the postwar international system, he was least enthusiastic about the role of the United Nations. During World War Two, the Prime Minister advocated a postwar structure composed of regional powers that would act to keep the peace in particular spheres of influence. "Several regional councils," Churchill once stated, "august but subordinate, . . . should form the massive pillars upon which the world organization [of the United Nations] would be founded in majesty and calm."[90] Yet, even during the war, when Churchill was, relatively speaking, most optimistic about the future of the United Nations, he was disinclined to put too much hope in an international body of this sort. Kenneth Thompson has noted Churchill's statement to Parliament on September 28, 1944, "in which he urged caution in putting forward grandiose plans for the postwar world."[91]

During the immediate several years after the war, Churchill grew further disenchanted with the organization. In May 1946 Churchill pointed to the problems which the Cold War posed for the United Nations.[92] In October 1947 he indicated that if the Soviets left the organization, no one ought to be unduly depressed.[93] As early as October 1948 Churchill was utterly disillusioned stating: "what should be the majestic centre of world security and later on of world co-operation and finally of world government has been reduced to a mere cockpit in which the representatives of mighty nations and ancient states hurl reproaches, taunts, and recriminations at one another, to marshal public opinion and inflame the passions of their peoples."[94]

Amidst all this gloom about the efficacy of the United Nations, a gleam of hope stands out in Churchill's thought in a rather surprising place. Churchill, among only a handful of international theorists, had some faith in the cultural route, or as Morgenthau termed it, "the Unesco approach," to international community. Morgenthau has explained:

> The philosophy of Unesco [the United Nations Educational, Scientific, and Cultural Organization] starts with the assumption that ... all activities that tend to increase contacts among members of different nations ... are factors in the creation of an international community and in the maintenance of peace. Implicit in this assumption is the supposition that nations are nationalistic and go to war with each other because they do not know each other well enough. ... Both assumptions are erroneous.[95]

Churchill, however, viewed the matter differently and publicly expressed his belief that a Unesco approach to forestalling international conflict might be helpful. In a speech in New York in spring 1946 he euphorically pronounced, "Misunderstandings will be swept away ... if the British, American and Russian peoples are allowed to mingle freely with one another and see how things are done in their respective countries. No doubt we all have much to learn from one another."[96] No doubt, but one would be hard-pressed to find the Political Realist who would put any credence at all in such a process.

All told, however, Churchill was much more sanguine about the prospects for a united Europe, perhaps even a United States of Europe, than about the prospects for a successful United Nations. In the immediate postwar years he saw the continent in an abysmal condition: "But what is Europe now? It is a rubble-heap, a charnel-house, a breeding ground of pestilence and hate. Ancient nationalistic feuds and modern ideological factions distract and infuriate the unhappy, hungry populations. Evil teachers urge the paying-off of old scores with mathematical precision, and false guides point to unsparing retribution as the pathway to prosperity."[97] Not only were Europeans suffering through postwar strife at home, but the brooding Soviet menace was lurking just beyond the continent proper. Both problems stood as important motives for some degree of unity.

Churchill's support for European unity was enthusiastic but qualified. On the one hand, Churchill scorned the naysayers and doubting Thomases. On October 28, 1947 the former Prime Minister told Parliament, "I believe that [European unity] can be achieved without injury to the national traditions, sentiments and character of any states, large or small, concerned."[98] Instead, he emphasized both the shared concept of Europe as much more than simply a geographical entity and the great advantages a united Europe could discover in a partnership with the British Dominion.[99] In 1950, speaking on behalf of a supranational united Europe, Churchill observed:

> People say that all these are visionary and sentimental ideas which ignore the practical realities. They say they blot out the lessons of the past and the difficulties of the present and thus will have no real application for the future. But it is a great mistake to suppose that nations are not led by sentiment. It takes too poor a view of man's mission here on earth to suppose that he is not capable of rising, to his material detriment, far above his day-to-day surroundings.[100]

On the other hand, the Prime Minister did qualify his support for European unity in certain key respects. He constantly stressed that the building of a supranational European state ought to be a natural process, beyond the confines of rigid federal constitutions.[101] In addition, Churchill generally conceived of Britain not as an integral part of the united Europe, but as a partner, a friend, and a sponsor.[102] As the Prime Minister remarked in 1953, "We are with them, not of them."[103] Moreover, the urgency that Churchill felt in the matter of European unity was intimately tied to his fear of the Soviets and his desire to create a strong deterrent to future aggression. When the British leader addressed the Council of Europe in August 1950, he put the task in the following terms:

> If in the next two years or so we can create a trustworthy system of defence against Communist invasion, we shall at least have removed the most obvious temptation to those who seek to impose their will by force upon the free democracies. This system of defence in the West will alone give the best chance of a final settlement by negotiation with the Soviets on the basis of our strength and not of our weakness. But there is not a day to be lost nor a scrap of available strength to be denied.[104]

With the rejection of the European Defence Community in 1950 and the dawning realization that European unity would be a project of decades and not of months or years, Churchill's enthusiasm waned. David Calleo has noted, "Out of office, it is true, Churchill was the father of Europe, but once back in power he did little to legitimize his Continental offspring."[105]

Notwithstanding these various qualifications, Churchill did support the concept of a United States of Europe with some ardor. Indeed, Anthony Eden claimed that Churchill singlehandedly revived prospects of a federal Europe with his Zurich speech in 1946.[106] Once again, his motivation was dual. At this point in history, Churchill believed that the stronger was continental Europe, the greater was the security afforded Britain. However, wholly apart from considerations of relative power vis-a-vis the Eastern bloc, Churchill the romanticist and idealist was attracted to the ancient shining ideal of a unified continent. In 1948, in another paroxysm of Wilsonian rhetoric, he stated, "The movement for European unity ... must be a positive force deriving its strength from our common sense of spiritual values. It is a dynamic expression of democratic faith based upon moral considerations and inspired by a sense of mission. In the centre of our movement stands a charter of human rights, guarded by freedom and sustained by law."[107]

Furthermore, in the quest for European unification, if Churchill harbored grave doubts as to the feasibility of the project, he kept his own counsel in the matter. In retrospect, even given a healthy degree of latitude for overblown rhetoric on the political stump, Churchill displayed a certain naiveté in underestimating the potential political difficulties of European union. It was not uncharacteristic for Churchill to declare that a non-united Europe represented:

> A horrible retrogression back to the Middle Ages. . . . *Yet all this could be ended in a single stroke.* Two or three hundred millions of people in Europe have only got to wake up one morning and resolve to be happy and free by becoming one family of nations, banded together from the Atlantic to the Black Sea for mutual aid and protection. *One spasm of resolve!* One single gesture! The prison doors clang open. Out walk, or totter, the captives into the sunshine of a joyous world.[108]

From this 'one-fell swoopist' attitude toward regional integration and from his early fervor for the cause of unity, it may fairly be deduced that Churchill at first saw no insurmountable obstructions to persuading the states of Europe to subordinate themselves to a supranational entity. This should come as no great surprise. After all, Churchill freely advocated any number of schemes that would require radical transformations of the foreign policies of states. Collective security was one such scheme; a supranational European state was another; world government stands as a third.

In curious juxtaposition to his deep pessimism over postwar international organizations such as the United Nations, Churchill was indeed hopeful that a united Europe might lead in the near future to a world government. At one point he argued:

> The creation of an authoritative, all-powerful world order is the ultimate aim towards which we must strive. Unless some effective World Super-Government can be set up and brought quickly into action, the prospects for peace and human progress are dark and doubtful. . . .
>
> If, during the next five years, it is found possible to build a world organization of irresistible force and invio-

lable authority for the purpose of securing peace, there
are no limits to the blessings which all men may share and
enjoy.[109]

Predictably, Churchill was hailed as a champion of world government for this observation and other similar remarks by Vernon
Nash, Vice-President of the United World Federalists, Incorporated,
and other world government leaders.[110]

In and of itself, Churchill's support for world government might
be seen as insignificant. Inis Claude has pointed out that the great
variety of motivations for this type of advocacy leads to a great
assortment of bedfellows in the movement.[111] For instance, one
can divide the world government proponents who truly believe
their schemes will, or 'must', work in the near future from those
who believe that merely striving for the ideal is a worthy cause.
Still others seem to believe that the West can rack up points in its
global competition with the Soviet Union by endorsing world
federalist ideas.

Not only are there any number of motivations for backing
these global plans, however, but a ritualistic declaration in favor of
world government is something that few international relations
theorists can refrain from making, before or after they treat the
serious issues in the field. Morgenthau himself has written, "Reforms
within the international society have failed and were bound to fail.
What is needed, then, is a radical transformation of the existing
international society of sovereign nations into a supranational
community of individuals."[112]

However, when Churchill's support for world government,
innocuous alone, is placed beside the other international schemes
he favored, a pattern of some significance emerges. Again, the
Prime Minister pays little heed to certain practical problems, problems clearly of great enormity, that stood in the way of these
visionary plans. For instance, while Churchill decried the attitude
of the Soviet government on the issue, he did not appear to
find even Soviet intransigence a hindrance to world government that was worthy of great consternation. Somehow, faith
alone would suffice. The British leader told the Congress of
Europe:

> We must do our best to create and combine the great
> regional unities which it is in our power to influence, and

we must endeavour by patient and faithful service to
prepare for the day when there will be an effective world
government resting upon the main groupings of mankind.
Thus for us and for all who share . . . our desire for peace
and world government, there is only one duty and watch-
word, Persevere.[113]

But, was this all hot air? Did Churchill truly believe the words
he uttered? The answer is 'most definitely'. Churchill, it is worth
reemphasizing here, was a man who spoke his mind. Martin Gilbert has written of the Prime Minister, "It was always his belief that
the truth should be made known, and that his criticism should be
in the open."[114] In 1937 Churchill wrote to Bernard Baruch, "I do
not feel that my own political position is much affected by the line
I took; but even if it were, I should not have acted otherwise. As
you know, in politics I always prefer to accept the guidance of my
heart to calculations of public feeling."[115] Surely this frank and
straightforward style hurt the Prime Minister politically on more
than one occasion. Yet, for the historian, this style also means that
Churchill's written or spoken words ought regularly to be taken at
face value. When the British leader endorsed a scheme like world
government, he was not merely talking through his hat. What the
Prime Minister said, he believed.

On October 14, 1947, Churchill again advocated a type of
world government, stating, "I believe . . . that above all these a
world instrument . . . 'to weld the democracies together', can be
erected which will be all-powerful so long as it is founded on
freedom, justice and mercy, and is well-armed."[116] To portray
Churchill as a Political Realist, one must lean toward dismissing
statements such as this as mere political sloganeering.[117] Perhaps a
more accurate view is to see in such a proclamation a helpful
insight into a cross-section of Churchill's theory of international
relations. Here, Churchill acknowledges the role of force in the
system: even a world government must be well-armed to keep the
peace. Here, Churchill repeats his belief that abstract ideals can
move states even to the extent of subordinating themselves to an
international body. Above all, in Churchill's very advocacy of the
notion of world government, the belief is plainly expressed that it
is not unreasonable to expect states to transform radically their
foreign policies.

This is a theme of supreme importance in understanding Churchill's theory of international relations. It runs throughout his statements on international politics. It underlies his confidence in the viability of collective security arrangements. It stands tall in his hopes for regional European integration. It forms the basis for his belief that in five years time a world organization of "irresistible force and inviolable authority" might be built.[118] It also helps to make clear Churchill's actions as a Cold War statesman.

Henry Adams once wrote, "The English mind was like the London drawing-room, a comfortable and easy spot, filled with bits and fragments of incoherent furnitures, which were never meant to go together, and could be arranged in any relation without making a whole, except by the square room."[119] It is tempting to join Adams, to refuse to struggle with Churchill's philosophy of international relations, and to compare his theory with the incoherence of a London drawing-room. In truth, however, while Churchill's thought was hardly 'of one piece', it was coherent — though not especially orthodox. Churchill was a man who could believe quite consistently that power dominated in the international system and that national forces might be harnessed in various visionary schemes: in collective security, in European unification, and in world government. While it might shock the pillars of the Realist school, an even-handed appraisal of Churchill's theory of international relations might well conclude he had a good bit in common with a man he much admired, Woodrow Wilson. Contrary to the protestations of the 'Wilson-bashers', this is not wholly a pejorative comparison. Perhaps it would be best, however, to set aside a critique of Churchill's philosophy of international relations for a few pages and first examine how the Prime Minister's theory was translated into action in the formative stages of the Cold War.

NOTES

1. Dean Acheson, *Present at the Creation* (New York: W. W. Norton & Company, Inc., 1969), p. 715.
2. Thompson has written, "The wisest analysts on the American scene have found in the words and political action of Winston Churchill the prototype of one conception of foreign policy. . . . Almost alone among postwar Western statesmen, he seized on the precepts of

political realism." Kenneth W. Thompson, *Winston Churchill's World View* (Baton Rouge: Louisiana State University Press, 1983), p. 17.

3. Winston S. Churchill, *Step By Step 1936–1939* (New York: C. P. Putnam's Sons, 1939), p. 25.

4. Winston S. Churchill, Vol. 1, *The Second World War: The Gathering Storm* (Boston: Houghton Mifflin Company, 1948), p. 210.

5. Thompson, *Churchill's World View*, p. 9.

6. Winston S. Churchill, *A Roving Commission* (New York: Charles S. Scribners Sons, 1939), quoted in Vernon Nash, *The World Must Be Governed* (New York: Harper & Brothers, 1949), p. 95.

7. See William Manchester, *The Last Lion: Winston Spencer Churchill* (Boston: Little, Brown & Company, 1983), p. 19.

8. As quoted in Louis Halle, *The Cold War as History* (New York: Harper & Row Publishers, 1975), p. 11.

9. Churchill, *Step By Step*, p. 26.

10. Ibid., p. 26.

11. *Parliamentary Debates* (Hansard) House of Commons, Fifth Series, Vol. 292, July 13, 1934, pp. 730–731, cited in Thompson, *Churchill's World View*, p. 103.

12. Thompson, *Churchill's World View*, p. 86.

13. Hedley Bull, *The Anarchical Society* (New York: Columbia University Press, 1977), p. 206.

14. Winston S. Churchill, *The Collected Works of Sir Winston Churchill*, Randolph S. Churchill, ed., Vol. 1, *The Sinews of Peace* (London: Library of Imperial History, 1975), p. 31. Note Churchill's broadly similar point made in The Netherlands on May 9, 1946. Ibid., p. 108.

15. Averell Harriman and Elie Abel, *Special Envoy to Churchill and Stalin 1941–1946* (New York: Random House, 1975), p. 360.

16. Rupert Emerson, *From Empire to Nation* (Cambridge: Harvard University Press, 1967), p. 20.

17. See Charles Bohlen, *Witness to History 1929–1969* (New York: W. W. Norton & Company, Inc., 1973), p. 167.

18. Churchill in Manchester, *The Last Lion*, p. 847.

19. Martin Wight, *Power Politics* (Harmondsworth, Britain: Penguin Books, 1979), p. 194.

20. Bull, *The Anarchical Society*, p. 219.

21. One might argue that the percentage deal proved beneficial in keeping the Allies out of each other's way while they intervened in third countries (for example, Soviet restraint while Britain extirpated the Greek Communists). Or, one might argue with Ambassador Bohlen that the concept of percentages was utterly meaningless in real life: how can influence be divided mathematically? Since the concept was never directly brought up again at Yalta or thereafter,

Bohlen argues it was a resounding failure. See Bohlen, *Witness to History*, pp. 161–165.

22. Kenneth W. Thompson, *Political Realism and the Crisis of World Politics* (Washington, D.C.: University Press of America, 1982), p. 96, by Captain Peter Thorneycroft. See also, Document 2 in Norman Graebner, *Cold War Diplomacy: American Foreign Policy 1945–1975* (New York: D. Van Nostrand Company, Inc., 1977), pp. 176–180.

23. Churchill, *The Collected Works,* R. S. Churchill, ed., *In the Balance,* p. 37.

24. Cited in Arthur L. Smith, *Churchill's German Army* (London: Sage Publications, 1977), p. 50.

25. Maxwell Philip Schoenfeld, *The War Ministry of Winston Churchill,* (Ames, Iowa: The Iowa State University Press, 1972), p. 243.

26. New York *Times,* November 4, 1953, quoted in Inis L. Claude, *Swords into Plowshares* (New York: Random House, 1961), p. 300.

27. Churchill, *The Collected Works,* R. S. Churchill, ed., *In the Balance,* p. 251.

28. Thompson, *Churchill's World View,* pp. 167–168.

29. Ibid., p. 251.

30. Churchill commented: "The argument is now put forward that we must never use the atomic bomb until, or unless, it has been used against us first. In other words, you must never fire until you have been shot dead. That seems to me undoubtedly a silly thing to say and a still more imprudent position to adopt." Ibid., p. 453.

31. Churchill, *The Collected Works,* R. S. Churchill, ed., *The Sinews of Peace,* pp. 20–21.

32. Ibid., p. 383. See his address to Parliament on October 28, 1948.

33. Robert E. Osgood and Robert W. Tucker, *Force, Order, and Justice* (Baltimore: The Johns Hopkins University Press, 1967), p. 259.

34. Richard H. Rovere, "Letter from Washington," *The New Yorker,* January 29, 1955, p. 74, quoted in Claude, *Swords Into Plowshares,* p. 300.

35. Winston S. Churchill, *Marlborough: His Life and Times* (Six volumes; New York: Scribner's, 1938), IV, p. 171, cited in Thompson, *Churchill's World View,* p. 85.

36. For a more detailed rendition of this argument, see Inis L. Claude, Jr., *Power in International Relations* (New York: Random House, 1962), p. 38.

37. Smith, *Churchill's German Army,* p. 37.

38. *Parliamentary Debates,* Vol. 310, March 26, 1936, pp. 1529–1530, cited in Thompson, *Churchill's World View,* pp. 167–168.

39. Claude, *Power in International Relations,* p. 9.
40. See Ibid., pp. 13-50. Claude distinguishes three primary meanings, each with several variants: the balance of power as a situation, as a policy, and as a system. See especially, pp. 13-15.
41. See Bull, *The Anarchical Society,* p. 101.
42. Osgood and Tucker, *Force, Order, and Justice,* p. 96.
43. Churchill, *The Collected Works,* R. S. Churchill, ed., *The Sinews of Peace,* p. 83.
44. Thompson, *Churchill's World View,* p. 232.
45. New York *Times,* October 15, 1947, p. 4, cited in Thompson, *Churchill's World View,* p. 248.
46. Churchill, *The Gathering Storm,* p. 208.
47. Ibid., p. 208. Could there not be a hint in the British leader's words that Britain's throwing her weight against the Continental bully was the right policy in a moral as well as a pragmatic sense?
48. Winston S. Churchill, Vol. 6: *The Second World War: Triumph and Tragedy* (Boston: Houghton Mifflin Company, 1953), p. 758.
49. Claude, *Power in International Relations,* p. 61. Supported also by Arnold Wolfers, *Britain and France Between Two Wars* (New York: W. W. Norton & Company, Inc., 1966), pp. 232-233.
50. The Prime Minister argued: "Theorists would claim that all shall be equally bound in principle and in degree in every case. To ask this is to demand more than mankind in its present development can sustain. To press the theme so far is to divorce it from reality." Churchill, *Step By Step 1936-1939,* p. 27.
51. Ibid., p. 27.
52. Ibid., p. 116.
53. Churchill, *The Gathering Storm,* p. 211.
54. Churchill, *The Collected Works,* R. S. Churchill, ed., *In the Balance,* p. 45. In this chapter we treat Churchill primarily as a political philosopher, in the next we note how Churchill turned theory to action in the context of the Cold War. Nonetheless, we might speculate here on whether or not Churchill, the statesman, would have allowed the abstract idea of collective security to dominate his management of British foreign policy. One might argue that Churchill paid lip-service to the concept, but would in fact have allowed the national interest, narrowly defined, to guide his policies. More plausibly, Churchill may have considered a functioning collective security system so beneficial that it was worth undivided support even at the expense of more immediate national interests. One somewhat ambiguous treatment of this issue is found in Wolfers, *Britain and France Between Two Wars,* p. 341. Wolfers manages to come down squarely on both sides of the fence writing: "[Churchill] advocated a policy of the national interest, in the traditionalist sense

of the term, but based wholeheartedly on a sanctionist League."

55. Arnold Wolfers, *Discord and Collaboration: Essays on International Politics* (Baltimore: The Johns Hopkins Press, 1962), p. 168.

56. Ibid., p. 119. Wolfers continued, "By the rules of collective security, the 'peace-loving nations' of the world cannot have too much power since they can be expected never to abuse their supremacy."

57. Thompson, *Political Realism*, pp. 191–192.

58. Halle, *The Cold War as History*, pp. 32–33.

59. Ibid., p. 32.

60. Wolfers, *Discord and Collaboration*, p. 119.

61. Claude, *Power in International Relations*, p. 39. Claude continued: "In this usage, it has no substantive content as a concept. It is a test of intellectual virility, of he-manliness in the field of international relations. The man who 'accepts' the balance of power, who dots his writing with approving references to it, thereby asserts his claim to being a hard-headed realist."

62. John Kenneth Galbraith, *A Life In Our Times* (Boston: Houghton Mifflin Company, 1981), p. 483.

63. Bull, *The Anarchical Society*, pp. 170–171. Bull also included minimizing international 'friction' as a major function.

64. In Louis Henkin, et al., *International Law: Cases and Materials* (St. Paul, Minn.: West Publishing Company, 1980), p. 184.

65. Churchill, *The Collected Works*, R. S. Churchill, ed., *The Sinews of Peace*, p. 133.

66. Harriman, *Special Envoy to Churchill and Stalin*, p. 549.

67. Mark A. Stoler, *The Politics of the Second Front* (Westport: Greenwood Press, 1977), p. 158.

68. Churchill, *The Collected Works*, R. S. Churchill, ed., *Europe Unite*, p. 203. Note that Churchill made a very similar observation on March 25, 1949. See, Idem, *In the Balance*, p. 37.

69. Idem, *In the Balance*, p. 83.

70. In Louis Halle and Kenneth W. Thompson, ed.s, *Foreign Policy and the Democratic Process* (Washington, D.C.: University Press of America, 1978), p. 79.

71. Churchill, *The Collected Works*, R. S. Churchill, ed., *Europe Unite*, p. 357.

72. Hans Morgenthau, *In Defense of the National Interest* (New York: Alfred A. Knopf, 1951), pp. 72–73.

73. E. H. Carr, *The Twenty Years' Crisis* (New York: Harper & Row, Publishers, 1964), p. 2.

74. William L. Neumann, *After Victory: Churchill, Roosevelt, Stalin & the Making of the Peace* (New York: Harper & Row, Publishers, 1967), p. 89.

75. Churchill, *The Collected Works,* R. S. Churchill, ed., *In the Balance,* p. 249.
76. Ibid., p. 35.
77. Thompson, *Churchill's World View,* p. 43.
78. Halle, *The Cold War as History,* p. 98.
79. Trumbell Higgins, *Winston Churchill and the Second Front 1940-1943* (New York: Oxford University Press, 1957), p. 5.
80. Churchill, *The Collected Works,* R. S. Churchill, ed., *The Sinews of Peace,* pp. 100-101.
81. Anthony Eden, Vol. II: *Full Circle: The Memoirs of Anthony Eden* (Boston: Houghton Mifflin Company, 1960), p. 217.
82. Thompson, *Churchill's World View,* pp. 120-127.
83. Thompson, *Political Realism,* p. 102.
84. Manchester, *The Last Lion,* p. 799.
85. Roy Douglas, *From War to Cold War, 1942-1948* (New York: St. Martin's Press, 1981), pp. 70-71. The Confidential Annex to the Cabinet Minutes of February 19, 1945 reiterate the same point: "[Churchill] was quite sure that Stalin meant well to the world and to Poland." (p. 73)
86. Ibid., p. 73.
87. Churchill, *The Collected Works,* R. S. Churchill, ed., *In the Balance,* p. 41.
88. Hans J. Morgenthau, *Politics Among Nations* (New York: Alfred A. Knopf, 1954), p. 5. Morgenthau claimed, "Nothing in the realist position militates against the assumption that the present division of the political world into nation states will be replaced by larger units of a quite different character." (Ibid., p. 9) One cannot help but wonder if what Morgenthau really meant was that the Realist position does not wholly and explicitly rule out radical transformations, though it certainly does militate against them. If statesmen do constantly pursue the national interest defined as power, as Morgenthau, the high priest of Realism, assures us that they do, it is illogical for Realists not to be, at the very minimum, pessimistic at the prospects of radical international change.
89. Ibid., p. 9.
90. Churchill, *The Collected Works,* R. S. Churchill, ed., *Europe United,* p. 270.
91. Thompson, *Churchill's World View,* pp. 298-299.
92. Churchill stated: "What happens if the United Nations themselves are rendered by an awful schism, a clash of ideologies and passions, . . . a vast confrontation of two parts of the world and two irreconcilably opposed conceptions of society?" Ibid., p. 317.
93. Ibid., pp. 303-304.

94. Churchill, The Collected Works, R. S. Churchill, ed. *Europe Unite,* p. 356.
95. Morgenthau, *Politics Among Nations,* p. 488.
96. New York *Times,* May 16, 1946, p. 2, quoted in Thompson, *Churchill's World View,* p. 29. Thompson noted that Churchill distinguished between potentially dangerous, superficial international contacts, like tourism, and more serious cultural exchange. (29)
97. Ibid., p. 67.
98. Thompson, *Churchill's World View,* p. 288.
99. Churchill, *The Collected Works,* R. S. Churchill, ed., *Europe Unite,* p. 66, 71.
100. Idem, p. 249.
101, Ibid., p. 348.
102. See, Geoffrey Parker, *The Logic of Unity* (London: Longman Group, Ltd., 1975), p. 168.
103. David P. Calleo, *Europe's Future: The Grand Alternatives* (New York: W. W. Norton Company, Inc., 1967), p. 169.
104. Churchill, *The Collected Works,* R. S. Churchill, ed., *In the Balance,* p. 352.
105. Calleo, *Europe's Future,* p. 169. Calleo goes so far as to compare Churchill and de Gaulle, writing: "Like Churchill, de Gaulle defeated seemed to be a good European. Both leaders proposed roughly the same confederal scheme. Each may well have expected his own country to be the leader." (p. 84)
106. Eden, *Full Circle,* pp. 32–33.
107. Lionel Curtis, *World Revolution in the Cause of Peace* (New York: The Macmillan Company, 1949), p. 59.
108. Ibid., p. 106. Italics in the original. See also, Churchill's speech entitled "United Europe Meeting" on May 14, 1947 in Churchill, *The Collected Works,* R. S. Churchill, ed., *Europe Unite,* pp. 66–73, esp. pp. 67–8.
109. Churchill, *The Collected Works,* R. S. Churchill, ed., *Europe Unite,* pp. 72–73.
110. See Nash, *The World Must Be Governed,* p. 182.
111. Claude, *Swords Into Plowshares,* p. 410.
112. Morgenthau, *Politics Among Nations,* p. 470. See also, generally, Chapter XXIX "The World State."
113. Churchill, *The Collected Works,* R. S. Churchill, ed., *Europe Unite,* p. 271.
114. Martin Gilbert, *Churchill's Political Philosophy* (New York: Oxford University Press, 1981), pp. 8–9. Gilbert recorded Churchill's statement in 1935: "No doubt it is not popular to say these things, but I am accustomed to abuse and I expect to have a great deal more of

it before I have finished. Somebody has to state the truth." (9)

115. Ibid., p. 10
116. New York *Times,* October 15, 1947, p. 4, cited in Thompson, *Churchill's World View,* p. 273.
117. See Thompson, *Churchill's World View,* p. 273.
118. See footnote 109.
119. Henry Adams, *The Education of Henry Adams* (New York: Random House, Modern Library Edition, 1931), p. 212.

CHAPTER TWO:

Winston Churchill
Cold War Statesman

I. Introduction: Prospects for Postwar Amity
II. The British Policy of the Second Front
III. The British Policy of Destroying German Power
IV. The British Policy of Occupying Germany
V. The British Policy Toward Poland

INTRODUCTION:

That the Cold War naturally developed into a great clash between the two postwar superpowers has largely obscured the significant role which other powers, particularly Britain, played in the first scenes of the drama. In fact, British relations with the Soviet Union deteriorated much more quickly than did relations between the two emerging superpowers. In 1949 Winston Churchill looked back on his country's relationship with the Soviet Union and observed, "Our differences with the Soviet Government began before the war ended. Their unfriendly attitude to the Western Allies was obvious before the end of 1945, and, at the meeting of the United Nations organization in London in January 1946, Anglo-Russian relations had already reached a point where the Foreign Secretary had to give the word 'lie' in open conference to Mr. Vyshinsky."[1]

Significantly, as late as Churchill's Fulton, Missouri address in March 1946, and for several months thereafter, no American officials would associate themselves with the Prime Minister's views.[2] Indeed, during this period in which Anglo-Russian relations rapidly deteriorated while Russo-American relations remained fairly amicable, a number of distinguished Americans, including General Walter Bedell Smith and Ambassador Joseph Davies were sent to try to convince the British Prime Minister to change what was seen in Washington as his obstinately anti-Soviet attitude.[3] In this task, none was notably successful. J. P. Morray put it well when he wrote, "Churchill did not engender the Cold War, but he presided over its delivery."[4]

As in the larger, later conflict, the miniature, preliminary Cold War between Great Britain and the Soviet Union had an air of inevitability to it. The history of British-Russian relations under the tsars as well as under the Bolshevik leaders suggested that any postwar cooperation between the two countries would be strained and fleeting. One author has commented:

> Against two powerful enemies, Napoleonic France and Imperial Germany, Britain and Russia had fought together as valuable allies. But in the century between these two wars their interests had clashed repeatedly and even produced one conflict, the Crimean War. . . . The Russian threat to the British 'lifeline' to India and to India itself, while composed largely of myths and misunderstandings, was deeply ingrained in British strategic thought.[5]

Not to be outdone, the relentless strategic minds in the Kremlin had long perceived the mirror image: a dire British threat to Russian interests in south–eastern Europe. All told, suspicions were mutual and friendships forced during even the best of times.

As for relations in the twentieth century between Great Britain and the developing Soviet state, a note of great hostility was struck at the outset and the situation never markedly improved. During the Russian civil war, Britain led the Allies in their support for White Russian forces. This support was no paper tiger on parade: British troops invaded Russian territory and occupied the ports of Archangel and Murmansk as well as the Caucasian oil fields.[6]

The activities of the Communist International in China, India, Persia, and Britain itself effectively barred any great rapprochement between the two countries in the 1920s. During the following decade, when the question of how best to handle Nazi Germany grew to deserving prominence, the governments of the two countries were consistently at odds in their policy approaches. When the Soviets urged containment, the British signed the Anglo-German Naval Agreement of 1935 and, later, agreed to appease Hitler at Munich. When the British urged containing Hitler through the threat of a two-front war, the Soviets signed their non-aggression pact with the Nazi government. Given the keen distrust with which the two sides were taken to viewing each other, it was fully in character for Churchill in 1944 to arrive in Moscow musing on "this sullen, sinister Bolshevik State I had once tried so hard to strangle at its birth."[7]

Alliances, the Comte de Ségur once noted, are "marriages followed promptly by divorce."[8] Yet, if the background for friendly postwar relations was hardly auspicious, the British-Soviet history was not in itself dispositive of the question of how the two countries would interact after the war was over. Certainly, the pressure of the historical forces which brought pre-war enmity was formidable; nevertheless, the degree of tension and hostility characteristic both of the miniature, preliminary Cold War and the later conflict itself was not entirely inevitable. That the forced friendliness of the war years would fade away may have been a foregone conclusion, but to find the reasons that estrangement turned to Cold War, we must turn not only to history, but also to the policies of the war years.

THE BRITISH POLICY OF THE SECOND FRONT:

The first British policy to have real significance in the growth of the Cold War was the decision to postpone a second front in Europe. Both allies embraced each other with great initial reluctance and distrust. The British feared the Soviets would eventually consummate a lasting separate peace with Hitler. Likewise, the Soviets suspected an Anglo-German agreement which would, in effect, force the two land powers to bleed one another while the British looked on from across the Channel.

As a demonstration of good faith, the Kremlin demanded three actions from the British: the transport of significant amounts of aid, the recognition of Russia's 1941 frontiers, and the establishment of a second front somewhere on the Continent. To Stalin, the lattermost action was the most vital. Establishing a second front would accomplish two objectives of surpassing importance to the

Russian dictator: immediate military relief and a long-term British commitment. The Soviets rightly believed that once a significant amount of British blood was spilt, Great Britain would be firmly committed for the duration of the fighting.[9]

In the event, of course, the second front was postponed for year after year while the Soviet Union gallantly defended against the great thrust of the Nazi offensive. Stalin's understandable, if overdrawn, skepticism at British excuses was further heightened by President Roosevelt's rash promise to Molotov that the western allies would certainly mount a cross-channel invasion during 1942. That Stalin was broodingly suspicious of Allied, and particularly British motives, is an understatement. When Churchill flew to Moscow in August of 1942 to inform the Soviets that no Anglo-American invasion would be forthcoming that year, he could compare the expedition only to "carrying a large lump of ice to the North Pole."[10]

Indeed, each subsequent postponement up to the eventual June 6, 1944 invasion, fully a year and a half after the great battle of Stalingrad, proved to be the scene for mutual recriminations. By the time the second front was ultimately established, Stalin was pleased finally to receive the promised aid. Nevertheless, the Russian dictator could believe—erroneously but understandably—that the British invaded, not primarily to aid their Russian allies, but to cut in on the spoils of victory. Surely one factor in the rapid deterioration of British-Soviet relations in the immediate postwar period was the legacy of mistrust resulting from the repeated quarrels over the second front.

Why, then, was Churchill so intent on stalling a second front? John Lewis Gaddis has written, "War Department planners regarded the Prime Minister's motives as blatantly political: he hoped, they believed, to let Russia defeat Germany while Britain used American resources to prop up the remains of its empire."[11] Here, the American officials surely misinterpreted Churchill's actions. Conceivably, Realpolitik might have dictated to a British leader the strategy outlined in the councils of the War Department. But Churchill was no Bismarck; much less was he a Machiavelli.[12] If ever there were an instance where duty, conscience, and honor beckoned a people to throw their weight into the fray, it was this war on the European continent. And, as Lord Moran, Churchill's physician and confidant, has pointed out: "On one point Winston has always been clear. He has reaffirmed it so many times that the very words have stuck in my memory: 'As a nation we want nothing; we will take nothing. We entered the war for honour'."[13]

The problems with establishing a second front, in Churchill's mind, were practical and tactical, not political, in nature. The difficulties were not simply conjured up to justify British inaction while the two great land powers bled one another. First, the Allies were undeniably weak in equipment such as landing craft and in divisions trained in amphibious landing. This was made abundantly clear to Churchill, well before Stalin's request for a second front, when the British Chiefs of Staff dissuaded the Prime Minister from a 25,000 man raid on northern Europe. As Joan Beaumont pointed out, "All the factors which had made Churchill's proposal for a raid impracticable—the shortage of shipping, the strength of German forces on the near coast of France, the lack of air cover further afield, and the need to conserve the anti-invasion force—still applied."[14]

On the tactical side, Churchill sincerely believed that trying to grapple head-on with the German *Wehrmacht* in the early years of the war was a strategic mistake. Again, this was no mere dust storm kicked up in an effort to obscure a British conspiracy against fully aiding their Soviet ally. On the contrary, Churchill's belief in an indirect, naval approach, oriented toward striking at the periphery of Hitler's Europe, was the product of generations of successful British campaigns. As one author has written, "With the disastrous exception of World War I, London had for centuries refrained from placing large bodies of troops on the European continent, correctly perceiving that land power, in terms of population if nothing else, was its weak point. Seapower, on the other hand, was the island empire's strength, and such power could most effectively be used in a peripheral campaign."[15]

Churchill's own experiences reinforced his faith in traditional British strategic thinking. He had personally seen the terrible slaughter of his countrymen trapped in the land warfare of World War One. As early as 1914 he had rebelled against "sending our armies to chew barbed wire in Flanders."[16] He looked for an alternative to the trenches and believed he found the master key in Anglo-American control of the air.[17] Furthermore, the Prime Minister was still fully convinced that the principles which had guided the failed Gallipoli expedition in the Great War would ultimately be vindicated. That expedition was a plan Churchill had himself conceived and stands as an example of peripheral strategic thinking of the first order. When Churchill stated in 1941 and for some time thereafter that military issues, not political or Realpolitik thinking, were uppermost in his mind, his words ring true. "My one aim," Churchill declared quite honestly, "is to extirpate Hitlerism from Europe."[18]

Pure as were Churchill's motives and sound as were his strategic considerations, the rationale for avoiding a second front must inevitably have seemed devious to Marshal Stalin. No one has ever censured the Soviet dictator for being an overly trusting soul. Moreover, Stalin had apparently believed for the better part of his life that the western capitalist nations were scheming to eradicate communism from the European continent. Though otherwise futile, the 1918 Allied intervention had established that the Soviet paranoia was not without some basis in fact. Beyond this, however, Stalin was a man whose strategic thinking was naturally grounded in the execution of large-scale land wars. To him, the British peripheral naval approach was as utterly foreign as it was natural for Churchill. Finally, the losses which the Russians were sustaining on the Eastern front were of such astounding magnitude that it is no wonder Churchill's strategic thinking seemed less than persuasive to the embattled Soviet leader.

At core, the controversy over the second front is another example of how easy it was for distrust to well up during wartime cooperation and later to poison the atmosphere in which postwar relations were being conducted. It also exemplifies how difficult it is to blame either leader for the view he adopted. Arthur Schlesinger, Jr., has neatly framed the Cold War in the following terms:

> The question remains whether [the Cold War] was an instance of Greek tragedy—as [W. H.] Auden has called it, "the tragedy of necessity," where the feeling aroused in the spectator is "What a pity it had to be this way"—or of Christian tragedy, "the tragedy of possibility," where the feeling aroused is "What a pity it was this way when it might have been otherwise."[19]

Taken as a whole, the Cold War surely has elements of both the Greek and the Christian tragedy. In the following chapter, the question of which tragic elements predominate will be explored.

For now, suffice it to say that the story of the second front was surely of the Greek variety.

THE BRITISH POLICY
OF DESTROYING GERMAN POWER:

The second wartime British action with real significance in the later deterioration of relations was the policy directed toward crippling Germany. No one can possibly quarrel with the overriding need to extirpate the Nazi menace. First priority had to go to eliminating Hitler's war machine in its entirety. The next issue, however, was how much power to leave with the postwar German state. The Allied decision to entirely shred German power is surely tied to the onset of Cold War. As Louis Halle has written, "The basis for the Cold War was laid when the two Western allies, the United States and Great Britain, looking forward to their victory, adopted the objective of utterly destroying German power and preventing its reconstitution for an indefinite future."[20] The policy of utterly destroying German power was most evident in two forms: the dismemberment plans and the unconditional surrender pronouncement.

In Churchill's thinking on the future of Germany, one can make out several distinct strands. One strand is his repeated plea that the Allies refrain from taking vengeance on the German people through lengthy trials and financial retribution. This strand seems to have grown to prominence, naturally enough, in the first years of the postwar period.[21] Churchill's words of 1949 were fairly typical, "I assure you you must forget the past. You must obliterate all parts of the past which are not useful to the future. You must regard the re-entry of Germany into the family of European nations as an event which the Western World must desire and must, if possible, achieve."[22]

However, to the extent that Churchill's sympathy for the German people—as opposed to their Nazi leaders—reached back to the war years, it in no way precluded his strong support for dismembering the German state. On the contrary, the historical record shows continuous support by the Prime Minister for splintering German power. In March 1943 on a visit to Washington, Anthony Eden commented, Churchill "has often spoken in favour of the idea" of dismemberment.[23] In November and December of 1943, in conversation with Stalin as well as at the Teheran Conference, Churchill endorsed in turn the proposal of Prussian isolation and confederation of Austria, Bavaria, and Hungary, followed by the more general plan to divide Germany into small units grouped together for survival.[24]

In September 1944 Churchill took his most famous step in favor of German dismemberment and embraced the Morgenthau Plan to pastoralize Germany. Sir Llewellyn Woodward reported, "The Prime Minister said in his telegram that at first he was taken aback by the proposal, but that he considered the argument about disarming Germany to be decisive; the beneficial consequences to Great Britain followed naturally."[25] Years later, Churchill repudiated the Morgenthau Plan telling Parliament in 1949, "I do not agree with this paper for which I bear, nonetheless, a responsibility, but when . . . fighting for life with a fierce enemy I feel differently towards him. . . . Anyhow if the document is ever brought up to me I shall certainly say that I did not agree with it and I am sorry I put my initials to it. I cannot do more than that, but many things happened with great rapidity."[26]

Surely, Churchill's last point is well-taken: no statesman running a project as large as the war effort staged by a major participant in a world war can be expected to act with great detachment and forethought in every instance. By the same token, however, Churchill cannot whitewash his record on German dismemberment with an *ex post facto* repudiation of the Morgenthau Plan. Churchill's support for the plan, as well as his later repudiation of it, must be read as part of the lengthy record of ideas concerning German dismemberment that cropped up throughout the war effort. The British Prime Minister endorsed practically every one of these proposals. For example, during the Moscow visit of October 1944, Churchill backed isolating Prussia as "the root of evil" and controlling the Ruhr and Saar.[27] Even as late as Yalta, in February, 1945, Churchill repeated his idea of detaching Prussia, this time with the corollary of establishing a large southern state with its capital at Vienna.[28]

Kenneth W. Thompson has written, "The Morgenthau Plan . . . ran counter to every sound principle of international politics."[29] Yet Thompson goes on to imply that Churchill's support for the plan was a mistake made in the frenetic rush of events during 1944.

This is too charitable. Not only was the Morgenthau Plan unsound, but all the proposals for German dismemberment were similarly unsound. The perspective from which German dismemberment made most sense was certainly not one based on balance of power, but instead was one based on collective security. Let us pursue this point a bit further.

Churchill recognized much earlier than most of his contemporaries that the next world war might be prevented by forestalling Soviet, not German, aggression/In September 1943 Churchill noted, "I think it inevitable that Russia will be the greatest land power in the world after this war, which will have rid her of the two military powers, Japan and Germany, who in our lifetime have inflicted upon her such heavy defeats."[30] A statesman intent on balancing powers against each other would have immediately stopped advocating German dismemberment. Yet, throughout 1943, 1944, and into 1945, Churchill was still strongly in favor of dismemberment plans. Surely this is logically and theoretically consistent only if taken as further evidence that the Prime Minister believed future peace depended on collective security, rather than on old-fashioned balance of power arrangements.

The practical implication of all this is that the critique of Allied policy advanced most notably by Louis Halle applies just as strictly to the British Prime Minister as to the American President on the question of German dismemberment. Both men thereby adopted the objective of utterly destroying German power. Neither man could propose an adequate replacement to fill the power vacuum thus created. To the extent that it had been possible to respond to the overtures of anti-Nazi Germans and establish a viable German government to succeed the Hitler regime, this aspect of the Cold War takes on elements of Christian, not Greek, tragedy. As the Allied leaders formed their policies in the waning months of the war, there was an alternative policy better suited to avoiding a Cold War than that adopted. It was not to dismember Germany, but to grant to Germans a legitimate anti-Nazi government. Only thus could the power vacuum have been avoided and the clash of East and West postponed.

Parallel to the Allied policy of German dismemberment was the policy of unconditional surrender. The policies were twin currents in the same stream. They sprang, in essence, from the same source—the world view that divided all people into two camps: aggressors and peace-lovers. Here again, Churchill shares responsibility, though again with certain ameliorating circumstances. In the Prime Minister's defense, it should be noted that the official public proclamation of the doctrine came by way of a surprise improvisation on the part of Roosevelt. According to Churchill, after the President publicly stated the doctrine, the necessity of Allied unity demanded concurrence from the British government. Several years after the event, the British leader endeavored to set the record straight before Parliament stating:

> I did concur [with President Roosevelt] after he had said it, and I reported the matter to the Cabinet, who accepted the position. Whether if we had all discussed it at home we should have proposed such a settlement is another matter. Still, [the Cabinet] did accept the position, as I, in my turn, on the spot, thought it right to do.[31]

However, pursuing this matter a little further, it seems unfair to pin all the blame on the American President. For Churchill, just as much as Roosevelt, was speaking of the German enemy in terms that logically suggested unconditional surrender. "We cannot yet see," the Prime Minister would characteristically thunder, "how deliverance will come or when it will come; but nothing is more certain than that every trace of Hitler's footsteps, every strain of his infected and corroding fingers, will be sponged and purged and, if need be, blasted from the surface of the earth."[32] If Churchill's tactics differed from his rhetoric, he could have easily made clear to the President in private what he really believed should be the Allied approach to the Germans. In fact, Churchill admitted precisely the opposite when he told Parliament in November 1949, "I have now looked up the telegrams and the records of the occasion, and I find that undoubtedly the words 'unconditional surrender' were mentioned, probably in informal talks, I think at meal times, between the President and me."[33]

The importance of this objective of the utter destruction of German power in its relation to the blossoming Cold War was not that it was actually carried out to the letter in practice. On the contrary, in a technical sense neither the Germans nor the Japanese surrendered absolutely unconditionally, without any assurances of any kind.[34] And, of course, the dismemberment of Germany into a number of small states never survived the planning stages. However, both of these Allied policies were indicative of the framework of thought favored by the western leaders. That framework of thought was of supreme importance.

It is deserving of reemphasis that this political mindset and policy framework did succeed in creating an absolute postwar power vacuum in Germany by stripping that country not just of the Nazi government, but of all government. The Allies preferred that no German authority at all be recognized in the conquered country. The result was that the vacuum was filled in the moment of triumph by the victorious armies and the stage was set for the onset of Cold War. By 1949 and 1950, when the western allies did support restoring German power under a moderate and anti-Nazi regime, the military boundaries had hardened, Eastern Europe was under Soviet dominance, and the Cold War had already begun. The crucial moment had long since passed. Churchill's own words ring truest here: "Want of foresight, unwillingness to act when action would be simple and effective, lack of clear thinking, confusion of counsel until the emergency comes, until self-preservation strikes its jarring gong—these are the features which constitute the endless repetition of history."[35]

THE BRITISH POLICY OF OCCUPYING GERMANY:

The period during which the western victorious armies filled the vacuum and occupied Germany was, of course, the most vital chapter in the developing Cold War. Contrary to expectations, this was not a period during which American and British policymakers saw eye-to-eye on how to deal with the vanquished Germans or the resurgent Soviets.[36] One result was that the British became isolated and distressed at the slim chances for postwar cooperation. As Churchill commented in a speech on Government Policy on December 6, 1945, "Abroad our relations with the United States have become more distant, and those with Russia more obscure. We are told the Big Three are never to meet again, which I heard with great grief. As for the five Foreign Secretaries who were to prepare so many things, all that seems to have fallen through. The condition of Europe is a nightmare."[37]

Now, the occupation period was not one in which Churchill was always in direct control of events. By July 1945 Churchill and the Conservatives had, of course, been voted out of office and replaced by a Labour government under the direction of Clement Attlee. However, Churchill's perspective on the unfolding European drama had remained steady from an early date. The policies toward the Soviet Union which he supported after leaving office were generally policies his administration had formulated years earlier. In short, Attlee's Labour Government approached the German occupation clinging tightly to Churchill's policy lines.[38] Thus, an examination of Churchill and the Cold War requires a brief sketch of the major dimensions of British policy in these key months.

The first noteworthy policy line concerned that old bugbear of how the Germans were to surrender to the Western allies. The unconditional surrender policy was most significant in creating a governmental power vacuum in Germany. Yet it was also important, in its application to surrendering German troops, for it directly created serious tension between the British and the Soviets. Churchill has been censured above for implicitly accepting the unconditional surrender mentality and has been deemed partly responsible for certain of the repercussions which followed. Yet, in tracing the development of the Cold War, one finds that the way in which the unconditional surrender policy was put in practice also had a significant effect on Anglo-Russian relations in the preliminary stages of the Cold War. Like one of those giant fish hooks sporting multiple barbs on which some unfortunate sea beast might impale itself, the unconditional surrender policy gouged and tore the Allies in a number of tender places.

To the extent that the unconditional surrender policy was not merely a reflexive backlash against supposed 'aggressor nations,' it was primarily intended to give the Allies a free hand in restructuring German and Japanese society after the war. However, secondarily, it was aimed at preventing variances in Nazi resistance to the different invading armies. Toward this end, the Allies pledged to demand that all German troops surrender before any one Allied force took significant numbers of soldiers into custody. As it turned out, this aspect of the unconditional surrender policy was chiefly in the interests of the Soviet Union since the Germans much preferred to surrender to the American and British forces in the west than to the Red Army in the east.

While the Americans stood fairly strictly by the terms of the unconditional surrender policy in this respect, the British clearly did not. Arthur Smith wrote, "The German Admiral [Karl Doenitz] had carried out a gradual surrender policy to the West instead of the unconditional terms demanded. The decisive element that allowed this was the willingness of Churchill and [Field Marshall Bernard] Montgomery to accept German military surrender of large numbers of troops in the final days of the war without demanding total surrender on all fronts as a precondition."[39] The numbers of Germans involved was large enough to cause serious concern in the Kremlin. Montgomery himself calculated that by May 5, 1945, 2.5 million German troops had surrendered to him along with an additional million refugees.[40]

The British motivations were twofold: realistic and idealistic in nature. First, Churchill and his lieutenants had for years forseen the possibility of war with the Soviets after victory over the Nazis. As early as November 29, 1943, Churchill had confided to Lord Moran that "a more bloody war" might be in the offing.[41] By the fall of 1945 Churchill believed a third world war could be discounted in the near future; however, earlier in the year the Prime Minister did not believe he could entirely exclude the possibility that the Soviets would continue to advance and force a confrontation with the western allies.[42] Under the circumstances, a gradual surrender policy that would result in British custody of over two million German soldiers with weapons was an attractive method of strengthening the British hand. Meeting force with force was always a cardinal principle of Churchillian Realism.

The other, equally great, motivation guiding British *de facto* acceptance of the gradual surrender policy appealed to the Idealist in Churchill. Quite simply, the Prime Minister's heart went out to the scores of refugees travelling to the west in order to throw themselves on the mercy of the western allies. These were people who loathed and feared the Communists as much as he himself did. Churchill was not only a chivalric Romanticist, but a moralist. Martin Gilbert has written, "In foreign affairs [Churchill] adhered to the view that morality must, in the last resort, be the true guide, and that moral forces did exist."[43] The moral and the chivalric demands of the situation ensured that Churchill would offer whatever assistance he could to the miserable fleeing refugees at whatever cost to Great Power amity. Consequently, not only did Montgomery allow a million of these poor souls to pass unhindered, but Schwesin von Krosigk later wrote that the British navy allowed another 1.25 million refugees to pass to the west on German ships in the closing stages of the war.[44]

Thus, on the one hand, the British under Churchill contributed to the development of the Cold War by embracing the unconditional surrender policy and must shoulder some responsibility for the larger implications of that act. On the other hand, the British under Churchill also contributed to deteriorating relations by refusing to carry out the unconditional surrender policy they had endorsed. This may have been another situation of Greek tragedy: a damned-if-you-do, damned-if-you-don't dilemma; however, let us reserve for the final chapter judgments on Churchill's theories and concomitant policy choices. For now, we might merely note the effect the Prime Minister's actions had on the burgeoning East-West conflict and move to the next policy line in the British occupation of Germany.

Martin Wight has suggested that from the Soviet perspective, the beginnings of the Cold War may be seen, in part, in the Allied "collusion" with the Germans during the last months of the war.[45] If 'collusion' is taken to mean active agreement to conspire to deceive or defraud, then the term is too strong to fit the Anglo-German circumstances. But there certainly was a degree of secret cooperation, perhaps left unspoken more often than not, between the defeated Germans and the victorious British. We have noted that while the Nazis were still fiercely resisting the Red Army in the east, the advancing British in the west accepted tides of surrendering soldiers and civilians. Stalin was too shrewd an operator to be duped by British obfuscation. He, too, knew just what was going on. Khrushchev remembered Stalin raging through the Kremlin bellowing, "Montgomery took them all, and he took their arms! So the fruits of our victory over the Germans were being enjoyed by Montgomery!"[46] But, what the British did with the surrendered Germans further unsettled the Russian dictator.

On numerous occasions in the immediate aftermath of the war, the Soviets claimed that the British were keeping prepared a large German force to fight the Red Army. It now appears that these charges were not entirely groundless. In a controversial speech delivered on November 23, 1954, Churchill stated:

> Even before the war had ended and while the Germans were surrendering by the hundreds of thousands, and our

streets were crowded with cheering people, I telegraphed to Lord Montgomery directing him to be careful in collecting the German arms, to stack them so that they could easily be issued again to the German soldiers whom we should have to work with if the Soviet advance continued.[47]

Did the Soviets catch wind of Churchill's plan? In his 1971 memoirs, Marshal Zhukov claimed the Kremlin knew about it all along.[48] Despite the fact that this is entirely *ex post facto* proof, the vehemence of Russian protests at the time suggested they did know something. In addition, the effectiveness of the Soviet spy network in the Allied camp strongly suggests that Zhukov's claim is accurate. If so, even though the memo was surely designed as a worst-case hypothesis, it could only serve to heighten Soviet mistrust of their British counterparts.[49]

The other ground for the Soviet charge of British collusion in retaining the German army concerned the *Dientsgruppen* and the administration in the British zone of occupation. Apparently, the British were conserving their own manpower by building up administrative structures composed of Germans. Surely this was innocent enough, indeed it was a tentative first step toward reestablishing a German authority in the power vacuum. However, the German personnel were almost exclusively drawn from the *Wehrmacht* and even paid according to former military rank. Arthur Smith pointed out, "The fact that Britain established the German *Dientsgruppen* in June of 1945, and continued to build their strength into 1946 was not in the spirit of Allied intent as expressed by the Potsdam Declaration and subsequent directives of the Allied Control Council for Germany. Additional suspicions were created by the fact that a significant proportion of the *Dientsgruppen* came from prisoners-of-war whose previous residences were on the other side of the Oder-Neisse line or in the Soviet zone of occupation."[50]

This review of British policies during the occupation of Germany is not meant to imply that the Soviets were blameless in this regard; nor that the British actions in every instance were unwise. What the British-Soviet byplay does demonstrate well is how readily the suspicions of one bloc can breed mutual suspicions in the other. When the two sides are forced into close proximity, as in the need to fill a power vacuum in Germany, the chances for tense relations increase exponentially. Again, the background for the unfolding drama is strongly reminiscent of Greek tragedy.

Furthermore, the story of the occupation of Germany reveals the dimensions of the miniature Cold War. Before the larger later conflict, an intense preliminary bout clearly took place between the British and the Russians. As Smith observed, "During the summer of 1945 there is little evidence of any Russian dissatisfaction toward the U.S. authorities in the American zone of occupation, and, in general, U.S.-Russian relations in Germany were still functioning fairly well. The same cannot be said for Russo-British relations, however, for in October on a London trip, Montgomery confided to Prime Minister Attlee that cooperation with the Russians in Germany had become simply impossible."[51]

But, Great Britain and the Soviet Union were not at odds solely because of the thorny German problems. It must be recalled that Britain, at the close of hostilities, still had the skeleton and soul of a Great Power. Though the shrewdest observers might have seen signs of future debilitating weaknesses, British statesmen still thought in terms of the global interests of their country. After all, in the immediate postwar period troops from the British Dominions occupied, or helped to occupy, Germany, Austria, Venezia, and Greece in Europe; Burma, Malaya, Singapore, Hong Kong, and other parts of East Asia, Indochina, and the East Indies; and Iraq, Iran, Palestine, the Suez and the Italian colonies in North Africa. All this in addition to the vast Dominion responsibilities, including the military commitment to India.[52] Thus, it is not surprising that British leaders saw their interests clashing with Soviet interests all over the world and not simply in occupied Germany. Yet for all the potential far-flung disputes, the next greatest conflict—aside from the German occupation imbroglio—was the clash in Germany's western neighbor, Poland.

THE BRITISH POLICY TOWARD POLAND:

If the British occupation policy represented one large burr under Josef Stalin's saddle, another great irritant chafed and rankled as well—the fate of Poland. The history of Winston Churchill and the Polish problem reveals with exceeding clarity how Churchill's political philosophy included a wide spectrum of different impulses. As previously observed, Churchill insisted that the British entered World War Two as a matter of duty, conscience, and honor. The declaration of war came two days after Hitler's invasion of Poland, and the stated justification was to honor the obligation to defend the Poles. Yet if the chivalric romantic impulses surfaced on the issue of Poland and the declaration of war, the calculating, realistic impulses came quickly to the fore during the war on the issues of the Katyn Forest and the Curzon line. As for the postwar period, when the issue was the composition of the Polish government, Britain under Churchill enunciated its policy toward Poland in alternating terms: first idealistically, then more realistically, then back and forth again.

Two great issues dominated Churchill's relations with the Poles during the war years: the Katyn Forest massacre and the Curzon line controversy. In both cases, Churchill dealt with Polish representatives in most realistic fashion. When the retreating Germans let the exiled Polish government know about the mass graves of Polish officers executed by the Soviets, the Poles naturally reacted violently and demanded an immediate full-scale investigation by the International Red Cross. This Churchill saw as interfering with the war effort. The Prime Minister hence buried his chivalric idealism and wrote Stalin promising to "oppose vigorously any 'investigation' by the International Red Cross or any other body in any territory under German authority."[53] Later, Churchill explained, "I had heard a lot about it from various sources, but I did not attempt to discuss the facts. 'We have got to beat Hitler,' I said, 'and this is not time for quarrels or charges'."[54]

On the tangled historical question of the boundary of the Polish state to the east, Churchill was no more yielding. The problem concerned the disputed land that extended beyond the territory that was settled entirely by people of Polish descent. In this disputed area were large and important Polish communities; however, the majority of the people were ethnically non-Polish.[55] When the Poles fought the Russians in 1920, the British Foreign Secretary, Lord Curzon, proposed at one point that an armistice line—not a permanent boundary line—be drawn. This, the famous Curzon line, had the effect of separating the disputed land from Poland.

As it turned out, however, the Russians and Poles eventually settled on an entirely different boundary, the Riga line, in their

Treaty of Riga in 1921. The Nazi-Soviet Non-aggression Pact contained a further line: the Ribbentrop-Molotov line of 1939. This boundary roughly followed the Curzon line, and the Russians, early in the war, began to claim that it constituted a fair boundary. On this issue, Churchill seems to have believed both that the Soviet claim had some merit and that, whatever abstract justice might dictate, the Poles were bound to lose under the circumstances. Consequently, when confronted by angry Poles pointing to the large numbers of their countrymen dispossessed by the Curzon line, Churchill adamantly told them that Poland must back down.[56]

When it came to dealing with the Soviets over the fate of postwar Poland, however, Churchill varied realistic with idealistic approaches. Walter Lippmann once wrote, "No nation, however strong, has universal world power which reaches everywhere. The realm in which each state has the determining influence is limited by geography and circumstance. Beyond that realm it is possible to bargain and persuade but not to compel, and no foreign policy is well conducted which does not recognize these invincible realities."[57] This was the type of realism with which Churchill closely identified. Roy Douglas has discovered a revealing paragraph that the Prime Minister apparently deleted at the last moment in a diplomatic exchange of letters with Peter Fraser, Prime Minister of New Zealand. The paragraph reads as follows:

> You do not seem to realize that Great Britain and the British Commonwealth are very much weaker militarily than Soviet Russia and in the regions affected we have no means, short of another general war, of enforcing our point of view. They are also far weaker than the United States, both financially and militarily. We are not, therefore, in a position to give clear, cool, far-seeing, altruistic directions to the world. We have to do the best we can. We cannot go further in helping Poland than the United States is willing or can be persuaded to go.[58]

However, Churchill was never one to confine his statesmanship to power politics. He understood that the statesman who thought only in terms of interest defined as power might miss opportunities to sway his international colleagues who thought, at times at least, in very different terms. As a result, Churchill tested the water with arguments about the fate of Poland which were far removed from

Realpolitik. Charles Bohlen, Roosevelt's State Department aide and interpreter, remembered: "[Churchill's] arguments were always well-reasoned but were often based on emotional appeal, which left Stalin cold. Churchill obviously felt deeply about Poland, the cause of the British declaration of war, and used all of this parliamentary skill and eloquence to plead his case."[59]

Lord Moran, too, has noted Churchill's tendency toward using both idealistic and realistic arguments in his discussions with Stalin about the problem of Poland. Moran observed:

> At Teheran in December the Prime Minister had obstinately affirmed: "we want nothing"—an attitude of mind not perhaps altogether appropriate to the transaction of business with Stalin. Whereas at Quebec, in the autumn of 1944, we find [Churchill] more belligerent; he had been driven to the conclusion that the only way to save a country from the Russians was to occupy it. A month later, . . . he was not so sure that such a policy made sense. He became certain that the only way to help the Poles was to make friends with Stalin. On his return from Moscow, the Prime Minister seemed to realize that he had got nothing out of Stalin and that Poland had been left in the grip of Russia. He lost no time in reverting to a more realistic policy.[60]

In the end, of course, Stalin remained unswayed. The idealistic arrows Churchill shot proved to be impotent, the realistic arrows proved absent from his quiver. This is not surprising. As Louis Halle wrote, "The reality of power politics was what counted for Stalin. . . . What counted for Roosevelt, however, and here Churchill followed him, was the idealism of freedom which might conflict with the reality of power politics. Under the circumstances, it is not surprising that . . . the ideal did not prevail over the reality of Stalin's unbalanced power in eastern Europe."[61] Yet for all the scoffing that the Realist camp might have showered upon Churchill for his supposedly naive, emotional appeals, the Prime Minister believed it important to make these idealistic arguments. First, that twin motivation of conscience and duty obligated Churchill to do his best on Poland's behalf. Whenever a country pledged its sacred word, it was obligated, in Churchill's mind, to discharge its responsibility as best as it might be able.[62] Second, Churchill and others believed emotional appeals might just work. Charles Bohlen later commented, "The appeal to Stalin's generosity was not, on the face of it, a bad tactic. It flattered his sense of power and gave him an opportunity to show magnanimity. But it did not work in this case."[63]

However, while the emotional appeal on behalf of postwar Poland and the composition and nature of its government was a tactic, it was not merely a tactic. Had Churchill's argument been put forward as a perfunctory, wholly strategic step taken simply because no other course of action was readily apparent, then Poland could not have been such a great irritant in Russo-British relations. In fact, of course, Churchill and the British did care deeply about the fate of the Poles. Their emotional and idealistic sense of responsibility affected them much more deeply than did any similar sense of responsibility affect that profound Machiavellian, Josef Stalin, and his cohorts. The fate of the Greek Communists, for instance, might well have moved a less realistic and more emotional man than the Russian dictator.

In the event, the deep British concern with the composition of the postwar Polish government played a significant role in the spiralling hostility between London and Moscow. It was no coincidence that in Churchill's 'laundry-list' telegram of complaints about Soviet behavior, drawn up on May 12, 1945, and sent post-haste to President Truman, the Prime Minister placed the Russian "attitude toward Poland" second on his list.[64] Halle has written perceptively:

> Having assumed too late an obligation that they could no longer discharge effectively, [Britain and France] now made the honorable gesture of attempting to discharge it. This obligation together with their inability to discharge it in the face of Russian ... opposition would involve them in the greatest embarrassment as World War II approached its end.... There is a sense in which the Cold War, like World War II, began with a Western attempt to rescue a Poland that was beyond its reach.[65]

One must not be left with the impression that the Russians were in any way blameless or justified in their actions in Poland in the aftermath of the fighting. Churchill made an excellent case that the Soviets had refused to retain " ... the spirit of Yalta, nor indeed, at points, the letter."[66] For his part, however, Stalin had made quite clear that Poland was a vital interest. In addition, while it is often argued that both sides at Yalta simply defined 'democratic government' in different ways, Stalin had clearly expressed his own definition long before. Bohlen reported the Russian dictator as saying at Potsdam, "if the government is not Fascist, the government is democratic."[67]

In truth, the clash between East and West over Poland boiled down to a clash between Stalin's hard-hearted realism, brutally looking out for the national interest of Mother Russia, and Churchill's honorable idealism, worrying about the implications for the post-war world of the Kremlin's brand of power politics. A man entirely comfortable with states pursuing 'interest defined as power' could hardly be much taken aback by Stalin's maneuvering in Eastern Europe. But, surely Churchill was not such a man. Indeed, in looking back over the record of Churchill as a Cold War statesman, one must be impressed with the importance of understanding the Prime Minister's theory of international relations in order to understand why the British leader acted as he did. The case of the delayed second front is ripe for misinterpretation unless one notes the duty, honor, and conscience theme that runs throughout Churchill's writings on international politics. Similarly, Churchill's long-time support for German dismemberment is practically inexplicable if one fails to observe that the Prime Minister believed that the future peace of the world depended on collective security rather than on classical balance of power arrangements. Churchill's support, hesitant though it was, for unconditional surrender is clarified by the fact that the British leader clung to a number of schemes based on the assumption that the world might be divided into 'aggressor' and 'peace-loving peoples.' In the case of the British policies in occupied Germany—the gradual surrender policy, the plans for using the German army, and the *Dientsgruppen* affair—one must be at a loss to try to explain Churchill's behavior as exclusively that of a particular school of theorists: his philosophy was an amalgam of realistic, idealistic, and romantic principles. Finally, the twists and turns of British policy toward Poland are navigable with some background in Churchill's theory of international politics. Given this close link between theory and action, we might now turn to a critical appraisal of Churchill as a commanding figure of mid-twentieth-century history. What is Churchill's place as a theorist and statesman in the Cold War era?

NOTES

1. Churchill, *The Collected Works,* R. S. Churchill, ed., *In the Balance,* p. 58.
2. William H. McNeill, *America, Britain, and Russia* (New York: Johnson Reprint Corporation, 1970), p. 658. Also, Herbert Feis, *Churchill, Roosevelt, and Stalin* (Princeton: Princeton University Press, 1967), p. 630.
3. See Arthur L. Smith, Jr., *Churchill's German Army* (London: Sage Publications Ltd., 1977), p. 81. Also, see Dóuglas, *From War to Cold War,* pp. 92–93.
4. J. P. Morray, *From Yalta to Disarmament: Cold War Debate* (New York: MR Press, 1961), p. 37. Earlier Morray argued: "The first period of the Cold War is dominated by the dialogue between Churchill and Stalin which opened with an exchange of messages on problems of Eastern Europe and closed with Stalin's retort to Churchill's Fulton, Missouri, address in March 1946. By this latter exchange, the most respected and most experienced leaders formally recognized that a state of Cold War existed between East and West. The steadily mounting acerbity in the tone of their public references to each other bespoke, and perhaps hastened, the steady deterioration of relations between the two blocs." (10–11)
5. William Neumann, *After Victory: Churchill, Roosevelt, Stalin and the Making of the Peace* (New York: Harper & Row, Publishers, 1967), p. 75.
6. See Joan Beaumont, *Comrades in Arms: British Aid to Russia 1941–1945* (London: Davis-Poynter, 1980), pp. 10–22, for a concise review of the misunderstanding and mistrust that characterized this relationship in the 1918–1941 period.
7. Winston S. Churchill, vol. 4, *The Second World War: The Hinge of Fate* (Boston: Houghton Mifflin Company, 1950), p. 475.
8. Neumann, *After Victory,* p. 87.
9. Stoler, *The Politics of the Second Front,* pp. 14–15.
10. Churchill, *The Hinge of Fate,* p. 475.
11. John Lewis Gaddis, *The United States and the Origins of the Cold War* (New York: Columbia University Press, 1972), p. 76.
12. See, generally, General Albert C. Wedemeyer, *Wedemeyer Reports!* (New York: Henry Holt & Company, 1958).
13. Lord Moran, *Churchill: Taken From the Diaries of Lord Moran* (Boston: Houghton Mifflin Company, 1966), p. 351.
14. Beaumont, *Comrades in Arms,* p. 29. Churchill first proposed a northern raid the day after the German attack on the Soviet Union.
15. Stoler, *The Politics of the Second Front,* p. 4.

16. See letter of December 29, 1914 in Martin Gilbert, *Winston S. Churchill,* Volume 3, documents, pp. 343–345, cited in Gilbert, *Churchill's Political Philosophy,* p. 61.

17. Churchill, *The Hinge of Fate,* p. 322. In supporting the British defense of India as one blow in his peripheral strategy, Churchill wrote: "Without active British aid, India might be conquered in a few months. Hitler's subjugation of Soviet Russia would be a much larger, and to him more costly task. Before it was accomplished, the Anglo-American command of the air would have been established beyond challenge. Even if all else failed, this would finally be decisive." (322)

18. Winston S. Churchill, "We Will Not Fail Mankind," January 17, 1941, *The Unrelenting Struggle,* ed. Charles Eade (London: Cassell and Company, 1942), p. 38, cited in Thompson, *Churchill's World View,* pp. 91–92.

19. Arthur M. Schlesinger, Jr., "Leninist Ideology and Stalinist Paranoia," in Thomas Patterson, ed., *The Origins of the Cold War* (Lexington, Massachusetts: D.C. Heath and Company, 1970), p. 106.

20. Halle, *The Cold War as History,* p. 32. Halle shortly thereafter concluded, "By the closing days of the War, then, at least as far as the Atlantic allies were concerned, statesmanship was exhausted, men were worn out, and circumstances had risen, at last, to full command. It is hard to doubt that, if statesmanship could still have averted the Cold War in 1942 after that it was too late." (41)

21. Perhaps the earliest public reference in this regard is contained in Churchill's speech on demobilization of October 22, 1945, in which he stated: "The test of holding Germany down will not be a hard one; it will be much more difficult to hold her up." R. S. Churchill, ed., *The Sinews of Peace,* p. 5. The earliest private reference seems to have been a statement to Lord Moran on September 13, 1944. See Moran, *Churchill: Taken From the Diaries,* p. 190.

22. Churchill, *The Collected Works,* R. S. Churchill, ed., *In the Balance,* p. 35.

23. Sir Llewellyn Woodward, *British Foreign Policy in the Second World War* (London: Her Majesty's Stationery Office, 1962), p. 441.

24. Ibid., p. 447.

25. Ibid., p. 471.

26. *Parliamentary Debates,* Vol. 467, July 22, 1949, pp. 1597–1598, cited in Thompson, *Churchill's World View,* p. 97.

27. Woodward, *British Foreign Policy,* p. 474.

28. Ibid., pp. 488–489.

29. Thompson, *Churchill's World View,* p. 96.

30. Winston S. Churchill, Vol. 5, *The Second World War: Closing the Ring* (Boston: Houghton Mifflin Company, 1951), p. 129.

31. Churchill, *The Collected Works,* R. S. Churchill, ed., *In the Balance,* p. 69. From a speech delivered July 21, 1949.
32. Manchester, *The Last Lion,* p. 33.
33. Churchill, *The Collected Works,* R. S. Churchill, ed., *In the Balance,* p. 138.
34. The Germans and the Japanese did sign acts of unconditional surrender on May 7, 1945 and August 15, 1945. Winston S. Churchill, *The Collected Works of Sir Winston Churchill,* Frederick Woods, ed., Volume 3, *The War Speeches: September 1943–August 1945* (London: *Library of Imperial History,* 1975), p. 435; pp. 512–515. Still, leaders from both countries were given certain clear and specific assurances before they signed. One man's assurance is another's condition.
35. Thompson, *Churchill's World View,* p. 344.
36. Arthur L. Smith, Jr. *Churchill's German Army* (London: Sage Publications, Ltd., 1977), p. 135. Smith commented: "The identification of United States policies with those of the British became so all-pervasive by 1947–1948 that the earlier period of differences, clouded by wartime expediencies, became blurred in popular thinking."
37. Churchill, *The Collected Works,* R. S. Churchill, ed., *The Sinews of Peace,* p. 44.
38. See D. N. Pritt, *The Labour Government 1945–51* (London: Lawrence & Wishart, 1963), pp. 68–69. Also, C. J. Bartlett, *The Long Retreat: A Short History of British Defence Policy* (London: Macmillan, St. Martin's Press, 1972), p. 12.
39. Smith, *Churchill's German Army,* p. 56.
40. Ibid., p. 70. See B. L. Montgomery, *The Memoirs of Field Marshal, The Viscount Montgomery* (New York: World Publishing Company, 1958), p. 319.
41. Moran, *Churchill: Taken From the Diaries,* p. 149. This early statement is corroborated by Smith who quoted Churchill en route to Teheran saying: "Germany is finished, . . . though it may take some time to clean up the mess. The real problem is Russia. I can't get the Americans to see it." Smith, *Churchill's German Army,* p. 37.
42. For Churchill's view on October 22, 1945, see Thompson, *Churchill's World View,* p. 207. Moran reported that the farthest Churchill would go on February 6, 1945, was to say that war was unlikely while Stalin was still alive. Moran, *Churchill: Taken From the Diaries,* p. 241. In May 1945 a Churchill telegram to Eden in San Francisco cautioned against the threat of world war with the Soviets. See, Smith, *Churchill's German Army,* pp. 71–72.
44. Smith, *Churchill's German Army,* p. 70.
45. Wight, *Power Politics,* p. 221.
46. See Smith, *Churchill's German Army,* p. 70.

47. Ibid., pp. 11-12.

48. See G. Zhukov, *The Memoirs of Marshal Zhukov* (London: Delacorte, 1971), p. 665, cited in Smith, *Churchill's German Army*, p. 15.

49. Smith mars an otherwise interesting, provocative, and well-documented book by greatly exaggerating the importance of Churchill's statement. He goes so far as to advance the hypothesis that on May 8 and 9, 1945, the Prime Minister was "on the very brink" of committing British forces with German troops in support against the Soviet Union. (79) A much more plausible interpretation was that these plans were worst-case hypotheses. Lord Alanbrooke supported this notion when he wrote on May 24, 1945: "This evening I went carefully through the Planner's report on the possibility of taking on Russia should troubles arise in our future discussions with her. . . . The idea is, of course, fantastic and the chances of success quite impossible." (Ibid., p. 77).

50. Smith, *Churchill's German Army*, p. 114.

51. Ibid., p. 93.

52. See Bartlett, *The Long Retreat*, p. 13.

53. Douglas, *From War to Cold War*, p. 19.

54. Churchill, *The Hinge of Fate*, p. 760-761.

55. Douglas, *From War to Cold War*, pp. 13-14.

56. See footnote 15, Chapter One. It was over this issue that Churchill had his noted exchange with Mikolajczyk.

57. Norman Graebner, *Cold War Diplomacy* (New York: D. Van Nostrand Company, Inc., 1977), p. 17.

58. Douglas, *From War to Cold War*, p. 87.

59. Charles Bohlen, *Witness to History 1929-1969* (New York: W. W. Norton and Company, Inc., 1973), p. 178.

60. Moran, *Churchill: Taken From the Diaries*, p. 221.

61. Halle, *The Cold War as History*, p. 70.

62. See Gilbert, *Churchill's Political Philosophy*, p. 107. Here Churchill expresses outrage at Neville Chamberlain's comment: "No pledge can last for ever."

63. Bohlen, *Witness to History*, p. 188.

64. Churchill, *Triumph and Tragedy*, p. 367.

65. Halle, *The Cold War as History*, p. 57.

66. From March 31, 1945 letter to Stalin, cited in Morray, *From Yalta To Disarmament*, p. 13.

67. Bohlen, *Witness to History*, p. 234.

CHAPTER THREE:

Winston Churchill A Critical Appraisal

I. Introduction: Critical Biography and the Cold War
II. Criticizing Churchill's Approach
III. Commending Churchill's Approach

INTRODUCTION

To isolate and to assess the thought and actions of any one man amidst the vast complexities of the Cold War is a task fraught with no little difficulty. At the outset, a most thorny dilemma is common to much biographical writing of this sort. On the one hand, Lord Acton's advice to young scholars retains its validity: the historian must be not only a judge, but a 'hanging judge.'[1] This tradition places a premium on decisive conclusions which blame or praise a leader for his part in the great currents of history. It was to this scholarly custom that Sir Francis Bacon bowed when he supposedly admonished his students, "it is far better to be wrong, than to be vague."

On the other hand, like a circus high-wire artist, the scholar must step cautiously indeed. Decisiveness unchecked can easily turn to disastrously excessive exaggeration. Hero-worship and scapegoating both must be shunned. Perhaps the latter error poses a particular problem for Americans. We seem to have demonstrated a peculiar affinity for a 'devil theory of history': a periodic attempt to trace great historical events to some single, prominent individual. Witness, for example, the noisy and diligent searches for the persons who 'lost' China, Eastern Europe, and Vietnam. While this national pastime makes for rousing public spectacles, the resulting historical insight—if any—is rarely penetrating. After all, what is the history of mere men and of today's events but, in Fernand Braudel's words, "a surface disturbance, the waves stirred up by the powerful movement of tides"?[2]

The first difficulty, then, formidable but not insuperable, is the tension between decisiveness and exaggeration in biography. One wishes to portray Winston Churchill neither as unduly heroic nor as unduly villainous. An event of the magnitude of the Cold War quickly reveals the absurdity of history by caricature. By the same token, however, one can hardly place Churchill firmly in the context of the Cold War conflict without coming to conclusions about the wisdom of his actions. Indeed, why bother at all with historical analysis that is entirely non-judgmental?

Not only does the historian treating Churchill and the Cold War face the delicate task of steering betwixt the Scylla and Charybidis outlined above, but he or she must also take account of the peculiar ambiguities of the conflict under examination. The Cold War is not easily analyzed in any regard. It is especially difficult to try to apportion blame, or, for that matter, acclaim, among the major actors. In fact, any one of the wartime or postwar leaders might easily be indicted for starting the Cold War.[3] It might have been Roosevelt for excluding the Soviets from the occupation of Italy in 1943 and from the secret of the atomic bomb in 1944. It might have been Stalin for his bellicose speech of February 9, 1946 and his walkout on the Marshall Plan on July 2, 1947. It might have been Truman for terminating Lend-Lease May 11, 1945 and for phrasing the Truman Doctrine in universalistic and possibly threatening terms on March 12, 1947. Just as conceivably, it might have been Churchill for stalling the cross-channel invasion to establish the second front and for confronting the Soviets in his Fulton, Missouri speech on March 5, 1946. With these and so many other possible events to seize upon, the historian invites trouble who aims to divide precisely the credit and the blame among the major leaders.

Indeed, how can one assess blameworthiness accurately in such an ambiguous conflict? Is a leader to be praised for pursuing a course in which 'cold' war did not become 'hot' war? Or, is he to be blamed for turning normal international relations into dangerously cold non-relations? In large part, one's answer must depend on prior assumptions about international relations theory. For instance, at the most fundamental level, given a distribution of global forces marked by two equally massive powers of hostile ideological bent, will peaceful relations be the norm and warlike relations the aberration or vice versa? Assessing blameworthiness requires a prior assessment of the dangers and opportunities of the circumstances. Kenneth W. Thompson has written:

> The paradox of the Cold War is that the rhetoric in which it is publicly explained and interpreted is the language of war: victory and defeat, good and evil, utopia and anti-utopia, black and white. Cold War policy, by contrast, is shaped by realpolitik, advance and retreat, testing and probing, and salvage operations, all of which fall in the gray area of partial gains and losses, limited advances and retreats, and the balancing of power.[4]

In this same vein, how is a historian analyzing a leader in the Cold War to handle an act which may have damaged relations between the blocs, but which was eminently defensible in terms of a higher good? For instance, the British struggle in Greece to eliminate the Communist revolutionaries may well have contributed to the development of the Cold War; nevertheless, in the view of Churchill and many others, the struggle was perfectly justified since it ensured that the yoke of communism did not fall upon the Greek people.

In short, despite evident temptation, the analyst cannot in good conscience make the presumption that forestalling the Cold War was the highest priority of each postwar leader. Plainly, such an objective was not—nor should it necessarily have been—the over-riding goal of any Cold War statesman. Whether it took the form of defending the values of liberal western civilization, of defending the Russian motherland, or of any number of other 'higher goods', all the leaders knowingly took actions that would clearly harm relations between the blocs. Simply put, dangerous as is a Cold War, many other dangers were and are considered worse.

The ambiguities and complexities of the Cold War have helped lead historians to treat the conflict as an almost inevitable development of the postwar international configuration. Louis Halle, for instance, uses the Cold War to demonstrate his point that: "The essence of history . . . is the contrast between the immensity of its movement and the limitations of the individuals who, often with the greatest gallantry, put themselves at grips with it."[5] This view is far from wholly mistaken. The saga of this peculiar conflict can, with fair accuracy, be told in the following terms: while neither superpower wanted a cold war, the flow of events moved inexorably in the direction of hostility between the blocs.

The reason for this inexorable movement was, in the first instance, the need, perceived or real, to fill the global power vacuums that stood out in the wake of the second world war. At times, perhaps, this movement was fueled by ideology; at other times by power politics or, simply, by human nature. In any event, one must wonder how much any one person could possibly do to stem the tide. Evan Luard, British politician and international scholar, has argued that this flow of events was not the consequence of misguided policies, at least on the part of Western statesmen:

> If Stalin had been met with policies of conciliation rather than with military strength in the years after the war, what would have been the effect? This was, in fact, to a large extent, the policy pursued by Truman and Byrnes during 1945 and the early part of 1946: U.S. military strength was largely abandoned and every possible effort was made to conciliate Soviet apprehensions. But it is doubtful if there was any significant difference between Stalin's policies at this period and at the height of the cold war five years later, when a United States policy of total deterrence had been substituted.[6]

Indeed, in an uncanny sense, Ralph Waldo Emerson may have foreseen the history of the Cold War as well as, more arguably, the history of the twentieth century, when he wrote, "Things are in the saddle and ride mankind."

However, while saddling the blame for the Cold War on any one individual or group of individuals is unsatisfactory, viewing the conflict entirely apart from the actions and policies of the leaders involved is equally unhelpful. Henry Kissinger has written, "The public life of every political figure is a continual struggle to rescue an element of choice from the pressure of circumstance."[7] To hold that in the Cold War the pressures of circumstance were tremendous is not necessarily to argue that the attempt to rescue an element of choice was always a losing and hopeless battle. While the choices of leaders may have been circumscribed and may have been dwarfed by circumstance on many occasions, policies were by no means entirely irrelevant.

Again, Schlesinger's challenge—choice versus inevitability; Christian versus Greek tragedy—masterfully frames the central issue. Again, perhaps the most reasonable conclusion is that in a conflict as variegated, ambiguous, and lengthy as the Cold War there were bound to be elements of both Greek and Christian tragedy. All told, the former elements predominate, but certainly not to the exclusion of the latter. Churchill himself made an acute comment on this subject, remarking to the House of Commons in June, 1946:

> The problems of the aftermath, the moral and physical exhaustion of the victorious nations, the miserable fate of the conquered, the vast confusion of Europe and Asia, combine to make a sum total of difficulty which, even if the Allies had preserved their wartime comradeship, would have taxed their resources to the full. Even if we in this island had remained united, as we were in the years of peril, we should have found much to baffle our judgment, and many tasks that were beyond our strength.[8]

One way to find a firm handhold when being tossed about by the eddies and whirlpools of Cold War historical analysis is to return to theory. Employing this method, we might ask how sound were the philosophical principles which Churchill was trying to employ in the period with which we are directly concerned—the years immediately before, during, and after World War II. If the theory was sound, but the objectives unattained, this might be taken as a leading indicator of Greek tragedy. If the theory was less than persuasive, then perhaps the unfulfilled objectives might have been attained through some other philosophical route translated into some different policy. In this situation, perhaps, the Christian tragic elements predominate.

CRITICIZING CHURCHILL'S APPROACH

"Political life," Churchill once remarked, "is a merciless affair."[9] In this pitiless spirit, we may be confident that our subject would himself never beg for quarter. Let us first, then, examine Churchill's philosophy of international political life for the peeling paint and rotten boards in the superstructure. Where was the Prime Minister's theory least sound? Where was his analysis of life in the international system least acute? Where was his philosophy translated to action least praiseworthy?

The most serious criticism of Churchill's theory might be that his faith that states could be expected to transform radically their foreign policies and subordinate themselves to a significant degree to higher institutions of various sorts is nothing more than wishful thinking. E. H. Carr has quoted Churchill saying in 1938, "There must be the assurance that some august international tribunal shall be established which will uphold, enforce, and itself obey the law."[10] Carr went on to comment caustically, "If Mr. Churchill had paused to ask *who* would establish the august tribunal, *who* would enforce its decisions, *who* would make the law and *who* would see that the tribunal obeyed it, the implications of this apparently simple proposition would have become apparent."[11] The evidence is indeed sparse that national leaders, or the people they govern, have the increasing faith in a supranational society necessary to justify subordinating their states to higher international institutions.

This general criticism may be applied with even greater force to Churchill's specific proposals. It is true in the case of world government, of a compulsory world court, of a wholly united Europe, or of an organized far-reaching collective security arrangement. In the latter-most case, the international organization which would be required to oversee and run a functioning collective security arrangement might have had some negligible chance of effectiveness in an earlier age, perhaps an age of different military characteristics and fewer and lesser nationalist ambitions. But to believe that a collective security organization was becoming a more viable alternative in the years after World War II is to completely misread the pertinent historical factors. Allow me to explain.

Inis Claude has written that collective security schemes were really designed for an earlier age of less military sophistication, when aggressors had to make elaborate early preparations for invasion and defenders had time to improvise plans for defense.[12] Today's covert operations and proxy wars, to say nothing of possible nuclear conflicts, have made collective security an infinitely more complex, and perhaps completely unrealistic, endeavor. Claude proceeded to point out that the diffusion of power of earlier ages has been replaced by superpower bipolarity. He wrote, "Collective security assumes a world in which every state is so vulnerable to collective sanctions that no state is free to commit aggression. This is certainly not the situation which has prevailed in the post-World War II period. . . . A collective security operation directed against the Soviet Union or the United States would be a major war, not a device for preventing such a war."[13]

As for Churchill's hopes for world government, one cannot but wonder if these were not only wishful thinking, but also ill-advised wishful thinking. Even if possible to implement, would world government be such a great step forward? Rupert Emerson has wisely warned, " . . . the easy course of cutting Gordian Knots with the paper sword of definitions is one to be resisted."[14] World government advocates fall into this very error when they define order as the imposition of government and conclude that in a world government there would be no disorder. Plainly, one may search in vain to find an instance in history where government entirely banished disorder.[15]

If the argument thus becomes that global disorder would decrease substantially if a world government were installed, one asks for the evidence or logic behind this conclusion. Of course, there is none. It is just as plausible to argue that global disorder would increase if all the nations and peoples of the world were bickering amongst themselves within the framework of a global government. Beyond all this, there is the danger that when power is concentrated it can just as easily be abused, and probably to greater effect, than when it is spread among the states of the world. The fact that a world government might conceivably exist ought not to be taken to mean that its rule would be any more just than that of any other government. 'All power,' we are told, 'corrupts, but absolute power corrupts absolutely.'

On a more ticklish level, Churchill's general quest for order in the international system deserves some comment. On the one hand, the theorist who bends his efforts toward eliminating or reducing war in the system must in the first instance be lauded. The hatred of war and the pursuit of peace is a praiseworthy theme that runs throughout Churchill's writings on international relations. But the keenest international theorists take full account of the fact that not all states have the same stake in the stability of the system as it happens to stand at any given moment. Surely, some statesmen will always be discontented with the current order. It is well worth remembering that to the discontented, the codewords used by the contented—words like revolution, disorder, and even aggression—do not carry the same negative or evil connotations.

To put it another way, the amount of sacrifice any people is willing to make to uphold the stability of the system is directly dependent on how beneficial the system is for them. To a certain extent, of course, Churchill grasped this notion. He never believed that conflict would be entirely eliminated, even under some future world government.[16] But one must wonder if Churchill did not overestimate the number of statesmen who shared his overriding concern with upholding the world order. Is it really possible, for instance, that enough states would put enough stock in retaining the current world order to make feasible one of Churchill's collective security schemes? Even less does it appear that enough states would treasure presumed gains in the world order highly enough to commit the self-sacrifice necessary to bring a world government into operation.

Even some of Churchill's less visionary and more practical ideas contain similar flaws in world view and logic. For instance, in setting up the United Nations after World War II, the Prime Minister highly recommended his regionalist variation in which the world organization would be composed of several great regional blocs. One might criticize this regionalist outlook from several perspectives. On the issue of the fundamental logic of this type of philosophical approach, Claude has written, "At bottom, the regionalist position is that the regional unit is capable of more effective organizational action than the global unit; the stress is placed here on the nature of the unit rather than the nature of the problem."[17] On the issue of whether the regional unit is naturally more efficient, one must remain skeptical. Again, Claude has pointed out, "Intraregional affinities may be offset by historically rooted intraregional animosities, and geographical proximity may pose dangers which states wish to diminish by escaping into universalism rather than collaborative possibilities which states wish to exploit in regional privacy."[18] Thus, in the case of regionalism, as in the case of world government, it is by no means self-evident that the idea in practice would be any great improvement over alternative schemes.

The final significant theme in Churchill's international philosophy which may deserve some criticism is his simplistic and arbi-
trary division of the world into aggressor and peace-loving nations.
Again, this thought lurked behind the Prime Minister's theoretical
advocacy of collective security and his practical application of
theory in the policy of utterly destroying German power. One sees
the same notion behind Churchill's idea that once an international
organization of strength was built that might deter the 'aggressor
nations,' then all that remains between man and an ideal world
order is the imposition of a just international realm of law. The
problem is that since all people carry within themselves aggressive
and pacific tendencies, the task is not so simple as to stamp out the
aggressors and then move on to other tasks. E. H. Carr has criticized Churchill's thought in a somewhat parallel manner in the
following perceptive quotation:

> The same fallacy is implicit in the once popular view that
> the aim of British policy should be "to rebuild the League
> of Nations, to make it capable of holding a political
> aggressor in restraint by armed power, and thereafter
> to labour faithfully for the mitigation of just and real
> grievances." Once the enemy has been crushed or the
> "aggressor" restrained by force, the "thereafter" fails to
> arrive. The illusion that priority can be given to power
> and that morality will follow, is just as dangerous as the
> illusion that priority can be given to moral authority and
> that power will follow.[19]

To expand on Carr's criticism, one might say that, theoretically,
any effective steps toward world order must necessarily include
both progress in marshalling power and progress in creating a
more just system. For effectiveness, the two must come together as
the two blades of a pair of scissors. The problem is not only that
one person's revolution is often another person's liberation, but
also that one person's just settlement is often another person's
unjust burden. Perceived injustice is at the root of much, though
certainly not all, 'aggressive' behavior; perceived justice is at the
root of much, though certainly not all, 'peace-loving' behavior. In
striving toward greater international order it is not always the
aggressive tendencies of the state involved that must be stamped

out; it is often the perception of the justice of the order that must be molded or manipulated.

Every aggressor is not a Hitler type, though some indubitably are. Power is necessary, but justice is necessary as well. The greater is perceived the injustice of the system, the more difficult is the task of marshalling the power of various states to uphold the stability of the order. If these intracacies and subtleties of world view were apparent to the Prime Minister, he did not often enunciate them. In sum, one might say that Churchill's theory of international relations was flawed, but not fatally so. The British leader, as previously observed, was not afraid to temper his idealism with pragmatism. Beyond this, he understood that the fundamentals of the international system are based on power. While idealism, emotion, and romanticism may have their valid niches, in the great conflicts of the system pious sentiment is useless. Force must confront force. With this basic perspective on the Prime Minister's thought in mind, let us finally turn to commending the deserving aspects of the man, his thought and actions.

COMMENDING CHURCHILL'S APPROACH:

On the other side of the ledger, there is much to be said in favor of Churchill's philosophy. First, that he had a philosophy at all is much to be admired. In his *Interpreters and Critics of the Cold War,* Kenneth W. Thompson has observed:

> Statesmen and scholars are tempted to assume they live and labor in similar worlds, but nothing could be further from the truth. The realm of the policymaker is the making of decisions and that of the scholar is the fashioning of principles and ideas. Statesmen, with but a few memorable exceptions, seldom are able to marshall their thoughts into any kind of coherent theory or approach.[19]

That Churchill had an articulable and original theory of international relations is an accomplishment that attests to the man's great talents. Not only was he a statesman, and a politician, and an historian, and a painter of no small ability, but he was also a legitimate international theorist. And, echoing Churchill himself, those who have a plan are in a much better position to act effectively in the world than those who trust to unspoken hunches and ad hoc policies.

Beyond this, however, Churchill indisputably had a good grip on the most important, most fundamental dimensions of the international system. He understood the significance of power in interstate relations and he grasped instinctively that upholding world order required the accumulation of deterrents to aggression. While the Prime Minister may not have been a Machiavellian, he rarely shied from the exercise of power. Power, in Churchill's view, was no unmitigated evil, whatever form it might take. Differences in power, for instance, might help to ensure an orderly world. All of these fundamental theoretical concepts, so readily grasped by the British leader, proved of exceeding benefit in Churchill's years of public service. In matters dealing with the employment of force in international relations, the Prime Minister's instincts were good. Here, his vision of the future—Britain's conflicts, enemies, and allies—was most acute.

As noted, Churchill's 'right way home' involved most basically the accumulation of deterrents against aggression complemented always by the vigilant and steadfast use of the diplomatic arts. With enthusiasm, we have acclaimed Churchill's instincts for power, qualified only by skepticism about his penchant for collective security. How about the latter half of the equation, Churchill's advocacy of diplomacy? On the one hand, perhaps the Prime Minister put too much faith in the degree to which a diplomatic settlement would ease the underlying conflict between the blocs. Might not such a settlement tend to paper over outstanding and irreconcilable conflicts to little ultimate purpose? On the other hand, despite this qualification, Churchill's great faith in diplomacy as an effective tool for the modern statesman was by no means entirely unjustified. If Churchill believed that a negotiated agreement might reduce tension, not altogether but to some degree, he was surely on firm ground. Were not tensions, after all, what the Cold War was all about?

President Roosevelt is supposed to have liked to say, "Try something; if it fails, admit failure honestly and try something else. But, above all, try something." In this spirit, Churchill approached diplomacy. The Prime Minister was a frank speaker and a tough negotiator, but he rarely if ever allowed his frankness and toughness to interfere with his willingness to bargain. What exasperated the

British leader above all else was 'frittering away' opportunities to reach a diplomatic settlement because of wildly unrealistic hopes for total surrender or because of a futile search for some elusively stronger bargaining position.[20] Whenever there was even the slenderest chance for a diplomatic agreement, Churchill made the effort to negotiate. As he told Lord Moran at one point, "I think I'd rather go and see the Russians. The country will be very disappointed if I give up trying to get the Russians in a friendly mood."[21]

We have also observed that while Churchill's philosophy evinced a certain degree of theoretical discontinuity, seen best perhaps in his variable approach to Stalin on postwar Poland, his philosophy also allowed for a good bit of practical flexibility. In many ways, Churchill was idealistic in the most favorable sense of the word. He was unwilling to divorce his direction of British foreign policy from morality. First, the Prime Minister believed that values could not be discounted internationally any more than they could be discounted domestically. More specifically and practically, he understood that states are led by sentiment in emotional, idealistic, and even romantic guises. He also held that for foreign policy to garner support in a democracy, a genuinely moral basis to policymaking is often an essential.[22]

Yet, as noted, if Churchill was an idealist, he was nonetheless unafraid to temper his idealism with pragmatism. One might say, in some ways, the British leader was a realist with a small 'r'. He would not allow idealistic optimism to blind himself to hostility from abroad, or to weakness at home. Amidst postwar celebrating, Churchill struck a very different note: "It is sad after all our victory and triumph and all that we hoped for . . . to find not peace and ease and hope and comfort but only the summons to further endeavours. But that is life!"[23] As for facing up to weakness at home, Churchill warned the British of their military deficiencies before and after both world wars and during the Cold War. After standing as one of the most inspirational war-time leaders in history, Churchill still could gaze unflinching at the debits as well as the credits of the war effort. In 1951, the Prime Minister remarked, "A mood of deep anxiety mingled with bewilderment oppresses the nation. They have tried so hard and they have done so well, and yet at the end of it all there is a widespread sense that we have lost much of our strength and greatness, and that unless we are careful and resolute, and to a large extent united, we may lose still more."[24]

In practice, this pragmatic strain meant that the Prime Minister often buried his idealism when the results of taking a stand upon it would be totally impractical or dangerously counterproductive. Churchill's conversations with exiled Polish leaders in London concerning the Katyn Forest massacre and the postwar Polish boundaries and government illuminate this principle in action. In addition, while Churchill was publicly criticized in Britain for allowing his enthusiasm to lead to half-cocked adventures, greater perspective now leads historians to suggest that this was in truth an unfair criticism. Evidence now indicates that the failed Gallipoli expedition in World War One was excruciatingly close to success when aborted by field commanders.[25] More representative of Churchill's generally levelheaded command was his postponement of the second front in the face of extraordinary emotional temptation to have at the Nazis.

For all of these credits, however, the sum of Churchill's philosophy somehow seems greater than its parts. We can count up the attributes of his theory, subtract various shortcomings, and discover at length that our gut reaction to Churchill as theorist and statesman is more favorable than the balance sheet might indicate. Why would most of us feel comfortable, in good times or in bad, knowing that Winston Churchill had the helm of our ship of state?

The clue to this paradox must lie in our simple and accurate impression that Churchill, above all, was a good man: moral, reasonable, responsible, and concerned. Ralph Waldo Emerson once observed, "Behind all true eloquence is a man." One must feel that behind all Churchill's actions and theories, was a man. He was a man unafraid to speak of cherished values. In 1936, for instance, the British leader eloquently defended parliamentary democracy in Paris:

> How could we bear, nursed as we have been in a free atmosphere, to be gagged and muzzled; to have spies, eavesdroppers, and delators at every corner; to have even private conversation caught up and used against us by the Secret Police and all their agents and creatures; to be arrested and interned without trial; or to be tried by political or Party courts for crimes hitherto unknown to civil law.

How could we bear to be treated like schoolboys when we are grown-up men; to be turned out on parade by tens of thousands to march and cheer for this slogan or for that; to see philosophers, teachers and authors bullied and toiled to death in concentration camps; to be forced every hour to conceal the natural workings of the human intellect and the pulsations of the human heart? Why, I say, that rather than submit to such oppression, there is no length we would not go to.[26]

Yet, hand in hand with espousing values came a mature realization of the staggering risks involved in upholding the values of western civilization in the twentieth century. Churchill regularly grieved to Lord Moran, that there might be a more bloody and disastrous World War III: "I believe man might destroy man and wipe out civilization. Europe would be desolate and I would be held responsible."[27] He was a man who put both freedom and human life at a premium and wrestled honestly with the potential conflicts between the two. What more can one ask of the soul of a theorist and statesman in the era of the Cold War?

NOTES

1. See Trumbull Higgins, *Winston Churchill and the Second Front 1940-1943* (New York: Oxford University Press, 1957), pp. vii–viii.
2. Fernand Braudel, *On History,* trans. Sarah Matthews, (Chicago: The University of Chicago Press, 1980), p. 3.
3. See Thomas G. Paterson, ed., *The Origins of the Cold War* (Lexington, Mass.: D. C. Heath and Company, 1970). Part III entitled "Whose Responsibility?: The Scholars Debate" features conflicting analyses by Arthur Schlesinger, Jr., William A. Williams, Melvin Croan, Adam Ulam, and Walter LaFeber.
4. Kenneth W. Thompson, *Interpreters and Critics of the Cold War* (Washington: University Press of America, 1979), p. xvii.
5. Louis Halle, *The Cold War as History* (New York: Harper & Row, 1967), p. x.
6. Evan Luard, "Conciliation and Deterrence: A Comparison of Political Strategies in the Interwar and Postwar Periods." *World Politics* XIX, 2 (January, 1967): 182–183.
7. Henry Kissinger, *White House Years* (Boston: Little, Brown and Company, 1979), p. 54.

8. Churchill, *The Collected Works*, R. S. Churchill, ed., *The Sinews of Peace*, p. 124.

9. Manchester, *The Last Lion*, p. 862.

10. Manchester *Guardian*, December 12, 1938, quoted in *The Twenty Years' Crisis*, pp. 178n–179n.

11. Carr, *The Twenty Years' Crisis*, pp. 178n–179n.

12. Claude, *Power in International Relations*, pp. 192–193. This basic argument is developed in much greater detail in Claude's Chapter Five "A Critique of Collective Security," especially pp. 192–200.

13. Ibid., p. 195.

14. Emerson, *From Empire to Nation*, p. 216.

15. See Claude, *Swords Into Plowshares*, pp. 411; 421; 428.

16. See footnote 116, Chapter One.

17. Claude, *Swords Into Plowshares*, p. 113.

18. Ibid., p. 114. It is interesting to note that on the subject of regionalism, Woodrow Wilson and Winston Churchill disagreed strongly. See Ibid., p. 121.

19. Carr, *The Twenty Years' Crisis*, p. 98. The quotation inside the larger quotation is taken from Churchill's *Arms and the Covenant*, p. 368.

20. Thompson, *Interpreters and Critics of the Cold War*, p. 4.

21. See Graebner, *Cold War Diplomacy*, p. 57.

22. Moran, *Churchill: Taken From the Diaries*, p. 488.

23. See Gilbert, *Churchill's Political Philosophy*, pp. 85–86.

24. See Thompson, *Churchill's World View*, p. 88.

25. London *Times*, October 3, 1957, p. 7, cited in Thompson's *Churchill's World View*, p. 90.

26. See, Manchester, *The Last Lion*, p. 20.

27. Speech of September 24, 1936, printed in Gilbert, *Churchill*, vol. 5, pp. 787–788 cited in Gilbert, *Churchill's Political Philosophy*, pp. 97–98. Gilbert quoted Churchill on another occasion as saying, "Short of being actually conquered, there is no evil worse than submitting to wrong and violence for fear of war. Once you take the position of not being able in any circumstances to defend your rights against the aggression of some particular set of people, there is no end to the demands that will be made or to the humiliations that must be accepted." (90)

28. Moran, *Churchill: Taken From The Diaries*, p. 151.

BIBLIOGRAPHY

Acheson, Dean. *Present at the Creation.* New York: W. W. Norton & Company, Inc., 1969.

Bartlett, C. J. *The Long Retreat: A Short History of British Defence Policy.* London: Macmillan, St. Martin's Press, 1972.

Beaumont, Joan. *Comrades in Arms: British Aid to Russia 1941-1945.* London: Davis-Poynter, 1980.

Bohlen, Charles E. *Witness to History 1929-1969.* New York: W. W. Norton & Company, Inc., 1973.

Braudel, Fernand. *On History.* Translated by Sarah Matthews. Chicago: The University of Chicago Press, 1980.

Calleo, David P. *Europe's Future: The Grand Alternatives.* New York: W. W. Norton & Company, Inc., 1967.

Carr, E. H. *The Twenty Years' Crisis 1919-1939: An Introduction to the Study of International Relations.* New York: Harper & Row, Publishers, 1964.

Churchill, Winston Spencer. *The Collected Works of Sir Winston Churchill.* Edited by Randolph S. Churchill. Vol. 1: *Postwar Speeches: The Sinews of Peace & Europe Unite.* London: Library of Imperial History, 1975.

_____. *The Collected Works of Sir Winston Churchill.* Edited by Randolph S. Churchill. Vol. 2: *Postwar Speeches: In the Balance.* London: Library of Imperial History, 1975.

_____. *The Collected Works of Sir Winston Churchill.* Edited by Randolph S. Churchill. Vol. 3: *Postwar Speeches: Stemming the Tide & The Unwritten Alliance.* London: Library of Imperial History, 1975.

_____. Vol. 4: *Marlborough: His Life and Times.* New York: Scribner's, 1958.

_____. Vol. 1: *The Second World War: The Gathering Storm.* Boston: Houghton Mifflin Company, 1948.

_____. Vol. 2: *The Second World War: Their Finest Hour.* Boston: Houghton Mifflin Company, 1949.

_____. Vol. 4: *The Second World War: The Hinge of Fate.* Boston: Houghton Mifflin Company, 1950.

_____. Vol. 5: *The Second World War: Closing the Ring.* Boston: Houghton Mifflin Company, 1951.

_____. Vol. 6: *The Second World War: Triumph and Tragedy.* Boston: Houghton Mifflin Company, 1953.

_____. *Step by Step 1936–1939.* New York: C. P. Putnam's Sons, 1939.

Claude, Inis L., Jr. *Power and International Relations.* New York: Random House, 1962.

_____. *Swords Into Plowshares: The Problems and Progress of International Organization.* New York: Random House, 1961.

Curtis, Lionel. *World Revolution in the Cause of Peace.* New York: The Macmillan Company, 1949.

Douglas, Roy. *From War to Cold War, 1942–48.* New York: St. Martin's Press, 1981.

Eden, Anthony. Vol. 2. *Full Circle: The Memoirs of Anthony Eden.* Boston: The Houghton Mifflin Company, 1960.

Emerson, Rupert. *From Empire to Nation: The Rise to Self-Assertion of Asian and African Peoples.* Cambridge: Harvard University Press, 1967.

Feis, Herbert. *Churchill, Roosevelt, Stalin: The War They Waged and the Peace They Sought.* Princeton: Princeton University Press, 1967.

Gaddis, John Lewis. *The United States and the Origins of the Cold War.* New York: Columbia University Press, 1972.

Galbraith, John Kenneth. *A Life In Our Times.* Boston: Houghton Mifflin Company, 1981.

Gilbert, Martin. *Churchill's Political Philosophy.* New York: Oxford University Press, 1981.

Graebner, Norman. *Cold War Diplomacy: American Foreign Policy 1945–1975.* New York: D. Van Nostrand Company, Inc., 1977.

_____. *The Age of Global Power: The United States Since 1939.* New York: John Wiley & Sons, 1979.

Halle, Louis J. *The Cold War as History.* New York: Harper & Row, Publishers, 1975.

Halle, Louis J. and Thompson, Kenneth W., eds. *Foreign Policy and the Democratic Process.* Washington, D.C.: University Press of America, 1978.

Harriman, W. Averell and Abel, Elie. *Special Envoy to Churchill and Stalin.* New York: Random House, 1975.

Henkin, Louis; Pugh, Richard, C.; Schachter, Oscar; Smit, Hans. *International Law: Cases and Materials.* St. Paul, Minn.: West Publishing Company, 1980.

Higgins, Trumbull. *Winston Churchill and the Second Front 1940-1943.* New York: Oxford University Press, 1957.

Kissinger, Henry. *The White House Years.* Boston: Little, Brown and Company, 1979.

Lacquer, Walter. *A Continent Astray: Europe 1970-1978.* New York: Oxford University Press, 1979.

Luard, Evan. "Conciliation and Deterrence: A Companion of Political Strategies in the Interwar and Postwar Periods." *World Politics* XIX, 2 (January 1967): 167-189.

Manchester, William. *The Last Lion: Winston Spencer Churchill.* Boston: Little, Brown & Company, 1983.

Moran, Lord. *Churchill: Taken From the Diaries of Lord Moran.* Boston: Houghton Mifflin Company, 1966.

Morgenthau, Hans J. *Politics Among Nations.* New York: Alfred A. Knopf, 1954.

_____. *In Defense of the National Interest: A Critical Examination of American Foreign Policy.* New York: Alfred A. Knopf, 1951.

Nash, Vernon. *The World Must Be Governed.* New York: Harper & Brothers, 1949.

Neumann, William L. *After Victory: Churchill, Roosevelt, Stalin and the Making of the Peace.* New York: Harper & Row, Publishers, 1967.

Osgood, Robert E. and Tucker, Robert W. *Force, Order, and Justice.* Baltimore: The Johns Hopkins Press, 1967.

Parker, Geoffrey. *The Logic of Unity: A Geography of the European Economic Community.* London: Longman Group, Ltd., 1975.

Patterson, Thomas, ed., *The Origins of the Cold War.* Lexington, Mass.: D. C. Heath and Company, 1970.

Pritt, D. N. *The Labour Government 1945-1951.* London: Lawrence & Wishart, 1963.

Schoenfeld, Maxwell Philip. *The War Ministry of Winston Churchill.* Ames, Iowa: The Iowa State University Press, 1972.

Smith, Arthur L., Jr. *Churchill's German Army: Wartime Strategy and Cold War Politics, 1943-1947.* London: Sage Publications Ltd., 1977.

Snell, John L. *Wartime Origins of the East-West Dilemma Over Germany.* New Orleans: The Hauser Press, 1959.

Stoler, Mark A. *The Politics of the Second Front: American Military Planning and Diplomacy in Coalition Warfare, 1941-1943.* Westport, Conn.: Greenwood Press, 1977.

Thompson, Kenneth W. *Interpreters and Critics of the Cold War.* Washington, D.C.: University Press of America, 1979.

_____. *Political Realism and the Crisis of World Politics.* Washington: University Press of America, 1982.

_____. *Winston Churchill's World View: Statesmanship and Power.*

Baton Rouge: Louisiana State University Press, 1983.

Wedemeyer, General Albert C. *Wedemeyer Reports!* New York: Henry Holt & Company, 1958.

Wolfers, Arnold. *Britain and France Between Two Wars: Conflicting Strategies of Peace From Versailles to World War II.* New York: W. W. Norton & Company, Inc., 1966.

Woodward, Sir Llewellyn. *British Foreign Policy in the Second World War.* London: Her Majesty's Stationery Office, 1962.

Zhukov, Marshal G. *The Memoirs of Marshal Zhukov.* London: Delacorte, 1971.